History of
American Education

From Harvard Scholars
to Worker Bees
of the New World Order

All Scripture quotations are from the King James Version of the Holy Bible.

Printed in the United States of America

ISBN 1-57558-47-0

History of American Education

From Harvard Scholars to Worker Bees of the New World Order

by Vaughn Shatzer

Table of Contents

History of American Education

For centuries, and up to the early 1960s, America had the most premier education system in the world—the envy of other nations. It served as a model for "developing" as well as "developed" countries.

Our children could read and write, add and subtract, and understand basic science principles. They also could recite historic speeches our Founding Fathers had given regarding our Constitution and God-given unalienable rights and freedoms. American textbooks taught the traditional basics from a Christian ethic and Christian worldview. The Bible was read to students every day, and Scripture was memorized. They prayed together, and taught and displayed the Ten Commandments (which established moral absolutes). Together schools, teachers, and parents followed the biblical admonition of Proverbs 22:6: "Train up a child in the way he should go: and when he is old, he will not depart from it."

Discipline was not a serious problem. The three top offenses were talking, chewing gum, and running in the halls.

Unfortunately, things have gone down a slippery slope since the early 1960s. Today we are truly in a public education crisis. This can be easily documented by test results and SAT scores.

Many have called this crisis the "dumbing down" of American education. What went wrong? In a nut shell, our former textbooks (which had taught the traditional basics with Christian values and principles) have been replaced with textbooks and teaching methods reflecting progressive ideas which are based on a humanistic and New Age world view.

A result of this worldly humanistic philosophy, according to the National Institute of Education, is the seventy-two million–plus American adults who are functionally illiterate. This means they cannot read or write above the fifth grade level. They cannot read a job application, a warning sign at work, a label on a medicine bottle, or count out correct change from a cash register. There are another twenty-six million who cannot read or write at all.

The top offenses in our public schools for the last few decades have been murder, drug abuse, rape, abortion, suicide, gang warfare, and sexually transmitted diseases, to name a few. As a whole, our public school system, as well as our society, is in a moral freefall.

The system based on traditional Christian principles and values worked. The current progressive system governed by humanistic and New Age principles has failed miserably. So the verdict should be obvious! Let's go back to what worked.

Unfortunately this possibility is not even being considered by most educational leaders. This suggests the existence of an ulterior agenda! Let's look at the agenda from a biblical perspective—going back to the beginning of American education—researching the foundations, principles, curriculum, and administration that was used for almost three and a half centuries.

The Pilgrims and Puritans arriving in the 1620s and 1630s were God-fearing individuals coming to America for the glory of God and the advancement of the Christian faith. These early settlers believed it was the parent's responsibility, not the government's, to provide godly education for their children.

They understood the biblical command of Deuteronomy 6:6–7: "And these words, which I command thee this day, shall be in thine heart: And thou shalt teach them diligently unto thy children." Ephesians 6:4: "And, ye fathers, provoke not your chil-

The Embarkation on the
Mayflower for America

(A.D. 1620)

dren to wrath: but bring them up in the nurture and admonition of the Lord."

America's first system of education was home schooling, modeled after the Holy Scriptures from Psalm 78. This psalm commands parents to pass on their godly heritage to the next generation. Parents would tell Bible stories over and over to their young children about God's strength and wonderful works. This was needful so that the children might set their hope in God and keep His commandments.

The children were taught from a book call the "Horn-Book." They were called horn-books because they were protected by a thin, transparent sheet made from an animal's horn. It contained the alphabet, the vowels and consonants, and then concluded with the Lord's Prayer. Ministers would usually tutor or teach the children. This would comprise a child's education until around age twelve.

The Pilgrims and Puritans realized that if their Christian values and principles were to endure, they must be transmitted to future generations. This was accomplished by starting the first school.

The name of America's first school was Harvard, founded in 1636. The Reverend John Harvard, a godly Puritan, donated the property and his library for the school. The official motto for Harvard was, "For Christ and the Church."[1]

Just like colleges and universities today, Harvard had certain requirements which students had to observe. One of the standards was:

Let every scholar be plainly instructed and earnestly pressed to consider well, the maine end of his life and studies is to know God and Jesus Christ, which is eternal life, John 17:3, "therefore, to lay Christ at the bottom as the only foundation of all sound knowledge and learning," everyone shall so ex-

Students at Harvard College were "to consider well, the maine end of (their) life and studies, is to know . . . Jesus Christ."

ercise himself in reading the Scriptures twice a day, that he shall be ready to give such an account of his proficiency therein.[2]

It is evident that Harvard's main purpose for each student was to know God, Jesus Christ, and the Holy Scriptures.

America, this was the foundation for your educational system.

Another requirement for students to be admitted to Harvard was to be trilingual in Greek, Latin, and English. The students had to be able to debate fluently in these languages. The freshman project for Harvard, Princeton, and Yale was to take a copy of the Greek New Testament and translate it into English in the student's own handwriting.

Many of our Founding Fathers such as John Adams, John Hancock, Samuel Adams, and Fisher Ames attended Harvard. Amazingly, Fisher Ames, who proposed the wording for the First Amendment, entered Harvard at age twelve.[3] Can you imagine being trilingual at age twelve, and graduating at age sixteen?

Harvard was not unique in its beginning. Princeton, Yale, William and Mary, Rutgers, and Columbia, just to name a few, had similar Christian requirements and standards. Of the first one hundred twenty-six colleges formed in America, all but three were formed on Christian principles.[4] Up until 1900 it was very rare to find a university president who was not an ordained clergyman. It is crystal clear that Christianity was indeed the basis of American education.

The first compulsory school law was in America was called "The Old Deluder Satan Act," which was drafted in 1647. The law began: "It being one chief project of that old deluder, Satan, to keep men from the knowledge of the Scriptures, as in former times. . . ."[5] The early American settlers still remembered the times in England when they were persecuted and kept from the knowledge of the Scriptures. To make sure this would never happen in America, the Old Deluder Satan Act was passed.

The law went on to explain that after the Lord increased the town by fifty families, a teacher was to be appointed to teach the children to read and write. The Old Deluder Satan law would be used in one form or another in our schools for more than three centuries. Sadly, after two hundred sixteen years of traditional Bible reading in our schools, the Scriptures were removed in the 1963 Supreme Court case *Engles v. Vitalis.*

Early American textbooks followed this same indoctrination of Christian principles. A prime example is the *New England Primer.* This primer was considered to be one of the most influential school textbooks in the history of American education. It was first printed in 1690 by Benjamin Harris, and was used in American homes and schools until 1900—that is two hundred ten years. Many Americans, including some of our Founding Fathers and U.S. presidents, learned to read, write, and spell from the *New England Primer.*

An eighty-page version from 1777, the era of our Founding Fathers, contains a picture of the Honorable John Hancock, president of the American Congress. Going through the *New England Primer* you can see the foundation of Christian principles that laid down moral structure in the important early years of training in the lives of boys and girls. The first section contained a rhyming alphabet, as the example following:

A—In Adam's fall we sinned all
C—Christ crucified for sinners died
D—The deluge drowned the Earth around
H—My book and heart must never part
Z—Zaccheus he did climb the tree our Lord to see.

Another section of the book contained the alphabet with Bible verses, as the example following:

E—Except a man be born again he can not see the kingdom
of God.

L—Liars shall have their part in the lake which burns with
fire and brimstone

N—Now is the accepted time, now is the day of Salvation.

Notice how salvation was stressed, as well as the reality of the
lake of fire.

One of the sections contains a test with one hundred seventeen questions used in the general studies of early learning for
the students. The example follows:

What offices does Christ execute as our Redeemer?

How does Christ execute the office of a prophet?

How does Christ execute the office of a priest?

How does Christ execute the office of a king?

Which is the fifth commandment?

What is required in the fifth commandment?

What is forbidden in the fifth commandment?

What is the reason annexed in the fifth commandment?

What are the benefits which in this life do accompany or flow
from justification, adoption and sanctification?

It is doubtful that students of today's high schools or senimaries could answer these questions, and it is certain they lack the
moral undergirding that this type of testing fortifies.

America's first educational system, first school, first school
law, and first school textbook, were based on the Holy Scriptures, God's promises, and Christian faith.

In the late 1700s our Founding Fathers realized, as had the
Pilgrims and Puritans, that if their Christian principles and values were to endure, then they must be passed on to the next
generation. This was accomplished by means of education. This

is the reason many of our Founding Fathers were directly in-volved in the educational system by teaching, writing textbooks, and making profound statements stressing the importance of a Christian education. The Holy Scriptures are to be used in ed-ucation as stated in 2 Timothy 3:16: "All scripture is given by inspiration of God, and is profitable for doctrine, for reproof, for correction, for instruction in righteousness."

George Washington, the father of our country, our first pres-ident, and one of our Founding Fathers, is a good example. He was home schooled by his godly mother, Mary Washington, who utilized Sir Matthew Hales book, *Contemplations, Moral and Divine*. His extending education was at the College of William and Mary. In the writings of George Washington of May 12, 1779, we see his educational philosophy. The Delaware Indian chiefs brought three of their youth to be educated in the Amer-ican schools. Meeting on the banks of the Delaware River, George Washington gave the following speech:

> . . . Congress will open the arms of love to them and will look upon them as their own children, and will have them educat-ed accordingly. . . . You do well to wish to learn our arts and ways of life and above all, the religion of Jesus Christ. These will make you a greater and happier people than you are. Congress will do everything they can to assist you in this wise intention. . . .[6]

George Washington made it clear that, above all, American schools would teach the Indians the religion of Jesus Christ.

Notice also who would assist in the teaching. Congress! On September 12, 1782, the first Continental Congress[7] granted approval to print ten thousand copies of a neat edition of the Holy Scriptures for use in schools.[8] That's correct! Our first Continental Congress had Bibles printed for our American schools. The printing was contracted to Robert Aitken of Philadelphia. The edition was known as the *Bible of the Revolution*. These Bibles were then used in the schools and by the people of the United States. Once again, we can see God's Word was at the center of our government and educational system.

Probably the most conclusive historical fact proving our Founding Fathers wanted religion and morality taught in the schools was a federal law signed on July 21, 1789, by George Washington. This law was known as the "Northwest Ordinance."[9] It was approved by the House on July 21, 1789, and the Senate on August 4, 1789. The Northwest Ordinance required territories west of the Ohio River who applied for admission as states to meet certain criteria. What is interesting and very important is the Founding Fathers were drafting the First Amendment at the same time they passed the Northwest Ordinance. Article III of the Northwest Ordinance provided for certain educational requirements before a territory could become a state. It stipulated they must teach religion and morality in the schools as well as knowledge. The exact wording declared: "Religion, morality and knowledge, being necessary to good government and the happiness of mankind, schools and the means of education shall forever be encouraged."

We can see from the Northwest Ordinance that our Founding Fathers believed that the schools were a proper place to teach religion, morality, and knowledge. How could the Founding Fathers pass a law requiring religion to be taught in schools—which at that time was Christianity—and then violate the First Amendment they had just passed?

This once and for all documents and settles, beyond a shadow of a doubt, that our Founding Fathers never intended or wanted a separation of church and state as has been defined by our courts in the last few decades.

Another prominent Founding Father involved in education

was Dr. Benjamin Rush. He was a signer of the Declaration of Independence. He was also a scientist who helped found five colleges. Dr. Rush wrote America's first textbooks in chemistry and psychiatry. In the late 1790s Dr. Rush authored a policy paper entitled *A Defense of the Use of the Bible in Schools.* He gives over a dozen arguments and reasons why the Bible should always be used as a textbook in the schools. Here are just a few:

> That Christianity is the only true and perfect religion and that the Bible contains more truth than any other book in the world. . . . The only means of establishing and perpetuating our republican forms of government is the universal education of our youth in the principles of Christianity by the means of the Bible.

What a statement!

A few decades later the American Tract Society took Dr. Rush's policy paper, *A Defense of the Use of the Bible in Schools,* and used it in the form of a gospel tract. This tract is still in circulation today, more than one hundred sixty years later. What a testimony!

As you read about the next Founding Father and his role in education, please prepare yourself for a shock. We have been taught and told by our courts and schools that Thomas Jefferson wanted a high wall of separation between church and state—that prayer, the Bible as a school textbook, the Ten Commandments, and the values and principles of Christianity are all unconstitutional. Let's document and research what Founding Father Thomas Jefferson really believed about education and schools.

While president of the United States, Thomas Jefferson became the chairman of the school board for the District of Columbia on July 17, 1805.[11] He wrote the first plan of education adopted by the city of Washington, D.C. The two principle textbooks used for the curriculum were the Bible and *Watts Hymnal*. We all know about the Bible, but what was *Watts Hymnal*?[12] The author, Dr. Isaac Watts, was a theologian, a poet, and famous writer who composed over six hundred hymns, including "Joy to the World" and "When I Survey the Wondrous Cross." His most famous work, *Watts Hymnal,* was on divine subjects collected from the Holy Scripture.

Thomas Jefferson also hired clergymen to be teachers. He personally contributed two hundred dollars.[13] On October 27, 1806, Mr. Jefferson granted two lots of government land for the first two D.C. school houses. These schools were led by clergy and were also used for church worship.[14]

In 1817 he founded the University of Virginia. The official motto for the university were the words of Jesus Christ in John 8:32: "And ye shall know the truth, and the truth shall make you free."[15] Mr. Jefferson had this scripture inscribed on the walls inside the Rotunda.[16] He also set apart space in the Rotunda for chapel worship. In 1898, seventy-two years after the death of Thomas Jefferson, the university would pass on this biblical admonition to the following generations. John 8:32 was inscribed in Greek on the frieze at the newly constructed Cabell Hall.[17] This Bible inscription remains today, reminding us of America's godly heritage.

It is clear to see that Thomas Jefferson had no problem with Bible verses being etched or used in the schools. He established the teaching of Christian history and the early church fathers under the history department. He also asked James Madison to compile a list of Christian theological books to be included in the university library.[18]

The most important set of books used by the university's law school were *Blackstone's Commentaries on Law.* Other prestigious law schools such as Harvard, Princeton, Yale, Kings

College (now called Columbia), and the College of William and Mary, also used *Blackstone's Commentaries.* These law books were used for about one hundred sixty years by American lawyers, courts, the U.S. Senate, and law schools, to settle disputes, to define words, and to examine procedure. Thomas Jefferson once stated that the influence of *Blackstone's Commentaries on Law* was so strong on American lawyers that they "were used with the same dedication and reverence that Muslims used the Koran."[19]

By doing research on the document, you can see what the law students at the University of Virginia, Harvard, Princeton, Yale, and others were taught from Blackstone's law books.

Sir William Blackstone, a Christian, was a renowned English jurist who lectured at Oxford. He wrote his famous *Commentaries on Law* in 1766, which opened with a careful study of the law of God as revealed in the Bible. In volume I, page 25, Blackstone states:

> ... When God formed the universe and created matter out of nothing ... [we can see the Big Bang theory refuted here] He impressed certain principles [or laws] upon that matter from which it can never depart. . . . If we farther advance to vegetable and animal life we shall find them still governed by laws but equally fixed. The whole process is not left to chance but is performed and guided by unerring rules laid down by the great Creator.

Here the theory of evolution is refuted. Blackstone continues:

> If our reason [or thinking] were always, as in our first ancestor before his transgression, clear and perfect, we would need no other guide. [Blackstone is referring to Adam here in the Genesis account of creation and the fall of man through sin.]

But every man now finds . . . that his reason [or thinking] is corrupt and his understanding full of ignorance and error. [Blackstone again refers to the sin nature of all men.] Therefore Divine Providence enforces its laws by direct revelation and they are to be found only in the Holy Scripture.[20]

Blackstone then closes this section with a very powerful statement: "No human laws should be suffered [allowed] to contradict these [the Holy Scriptures]."[21] In other words, man's laws could never contradict God's laws written in the Holy Scriptures. If man's laws did contradict God's laws, Blackstone stated that "they were not valid." The Scriptures affirm this in Acts 5:29: "We ought to obey God rather than men."

How many laws can you think of in America that contradict God's laws?

One other section in the sixteen hundred pages of *Blackstone's Commentaries* that American law students were taught was entitled "The Nature of Crimes and Their Punishment." In this section, the crime was named with the punishment, and then a footnote at the bottom of the page gave the reference from the Holy Scriptures. The following are just a few examples:

Murder—Genesis 9:6 and Numbers 35:31[22]
Rape—Deuteronomy 22:25[23]
Kidnapping—Exodus 21:16[24]

Blackstone had a great deal to say about the "crime against nature." Sadly, it is no longer enforced today because this crime is now called "gay rights." What did our first American law books teach students about the crime against nature?

This . . . crime is the more detestable . . . and . . . of a still deeper malignity; the crime against nature, committed either with man or beast . . . the very mention of . . . [the crime against nature] . . . is a disgrace to human nature . . . a crime not fit to be named. Which leads me to add a word concerning its punishment.[25]

. . . This is the voice of nature and of reason and the express law of God determined to be capital.[26] Lev. 20:13–15: "If a man also lie with mankind, as he lieth with a woman, both of them have committed an abomination: they shall surely be put to death; their blood shall be upon them. . . . And if a man lie with a beast, he shall surely be put to death: and ye shall slay the beast."

Blackstone now gives an example from Genesis 19.

We have a single instance long before the Jewish dispensation by the destruction of two cities, Sodom and Gomorrah, with fire from heaven; so, this is a universal precept.[27]

Blackstone goes on to say the crime against nature should be treated as a felony. Once law students read the footnotes from *Blackstone's Commentaries* they understood there were moral absolutes straight from the Holy Scriptures—absolutes that would never change.

From this documented evidence, it is plain to see that Thomas Jefferson did approve and institute the Bible and Christian principles into the American education system.

Concerning education, the last and most famous Founding Father is Noah Webster. He earned the title "Schoolmaster of our Republic." Mr. Webster graduated from Yale University, was an expert in grammar, and had mastered twenty-eight languages. His academic and professional credentials are very extensive. He wrote many school textbooks, the most famous being the *1828 American Dictionary of the English Language.* In less than two decades, twenty-four million copies of his dictionaries had been purchased by schools and the public.[28] This dictionary, the grandfather of all dictionaries, defined many words biblically and used scriptural references. Here is just one example: "Truth—Conformity to fact or reality." He then lists Bible verses for the exact meaning.

1) Thy Word is truth—John 17.
2) Jesus Christ is called the truth—John 14.
3) To do truth is to practice what God commands—John 3.

Boys and girls were taught that the Word of God and Jesus Christ is truth. Sadly, our students today are being taught that truth is subjective. There are now situation ethics, values clarification, alternative lifestyles, and let us not forget the term "politically correct."

The 1854 edition of Noah Webster's dictionary gave his personal testimony of how he was converted to Christ.

. . . that "salvation must be wholly of grace." . . . He felt constrained to cast himself down before God, confess his sins, implore pardon through the merits of the Redeemer. He made a public profession of religion in April 1808.[29]

When Noah Webster was in his eighties a terminal sickness came upon him. Here are his parting words, which were printed in his 1854 dictionary.

He expressed his entire resignation to the will of God and his unshaken trust in the atoning blood of the Redeemer. "I know in whom I have believed and that He is able to keep that which I have committed to him against that day."[30]

Mr. Webster went home to be with his Savior and Lord on June 25, 1847.

Modern Webster's dictionaries do not contain biblical definitions, Bible verses, or Webster's personal testimony of receiving Jesus Christ. Revisionists and censors have removed the thousands of scripture references and biblical definitions. Basically they have replaced them with humanistic thoughts. Noah Webster's original dictionary, along with many of the reprints, would be banned in the public schools today due to the myth of separation of church and state.

Mr. Webster believed that Christianity was very important to education and to government. He stated:

> The Christian religion is the most important and one of the first things in which all children, under a free government, ought to be instructed. . . . No truth is more evident to my mind than that the Christian religion must be the basis of any government intended to secure the rights and privileges of a free people.[31]

Another famous book written by Noah Webster was his *Blue-Backed Speller*. It did more for American education than any other single book, except the Bible. This speller was first written in 1783 and used as the national standard for American schools until 1930—almost one and one-half centuries. It sold a million copies a year for one hundred years (that is one hundred million copies). This 175-page elementary speller started with one-syllable words and worked up to seven-syllable words. The spelling words were then put into a sentence.

> Preach—The preacher is to preach the gospel.
> Loaf—The man who drinks rum will soon want a loaf of bread.

Create—God created the heavens and earth in six days.

Disgrace—The drunkards face will publish his vice and his disgrace.

Consent—If sinners entice thee, consent thou not.

Mediator—Christ is the mediator between an offended God and offending man.

Adversary—The devil is the great adversary of man.

Intoxicate—Liquors that intoxicate are to be avoided as poison.

See if you can spell the following elementary words:

loquacious
sagacious
mucilaginous
legerdemain
duodecimo
imperceptibility
perpendicularity
incomprehensibility

The final portion of the *Blue-Backed Speller* has short stories with morals such as "The Partial Judge," "The Cat and the Rat," "The Bear and the Two friends," and "The Boy That Stole Apples." The story of the boy that stole apples follows:

An old man found a rude boy upon one of his trees stealing apples, and desired him to come down, but the young saucebox told him plainly he would not. "Won't you?" said the old man, "Then I will fetch you down," so he pulled up some turf or grass and threw at him; but this only made the youngster laugh, to think the old man should pretend to beat him down from the tree with grass only.

"Well, well," said the old man, "If neither words nor grass will do, I must try what virtue there is in stones," so the old man pelted him heartily with stones, which soon made the young chap hasten down from the tree and beg the old man's pardon. Moral of the story—if good words and gentle means will not reclaim the wicked, they must be dealt with in a more severe manner.

Noah Webster wrote another very important history and government textbook entitled *History of the United States*. In this text he explains to students where the principles to our republican form of government and U.S. Constitution are found. Mr. Webster explained:

> The brief exposition of the constitution of the United States, will unfold to young persons the principles of republican government; and it is the sincere desire of the writer that our citizens should early understand that the genuine source of correct republican principles is the Bible, particularly the New Testament or the Christian religion.[32]

The Bible is the source for our principles in our republican form of government. Mr. Webster was quite an authority on government because he helped write Articles 1, Section 8, of our U.S. Constitution, served nine terms in the Connecticut legislature, three terms in the Massachusetts legislature, four terms as judge, and was one of the first to call for a Constitutional Convention.

Unfortunately, most students and American citizens think we are a democracy. Remember, when we pledge allegiance to the flag, we also pledge allegiance to the republic for which it stands, not to the democracy for which it stands. Article 4, section 4, of our U.S. Constitution "shall guarantee to every state . . . a republican form of government."

Our Founding Fathers made it clear that we were not (and hopefully never would become) a democracy. Here are some of their statements concerning a democracy.

John Adams: "Remember, democracy never lasts long. It soon wastes, exhausts, and murders itself. There never was a democracy yet that did not commit suicide."[33]

James Madison: "Democracies have ever been spectacles of turbulence and contention; have ever been found incompatible with personal security, or the rights of property...."[34]

Dr. Benjamin Rush described a democracy as a "mobocracy" and the "devil's own government."[35]

Why did the Founding Fathers detest a democracy? Because in a true democracy there are no absolutes, and the majority of votes on any issue wins. Here is an example: If the majority (fifty-one percent) of the people in a democracy decide murder is no longer a crime, it will no longer be a crime. In our republic, murder is always a crime because a republic is ruled by laws. Whose laws?

Recall Noah Webster and Dr. Benjamin Rush stated that the source of republican principles was the Bible, particularly the New Testament or the Christian religion. Therefore, in a republic murder is a crime because murder is always a crime in the Word of God.

To be sure these Christian principles and values of government were not lost or forgotten, many of our Founding Fathers became educators and wrote school textbooks like *History of the United States.* In *History of the United States,* Noah Webster gave his students another reason why the Bible must be the basis of our government.

The moral principles and precepts contained in the Scriptures ought to form the basis of all our civil constitutions and laws . . . all the miseries and evils which man suffer from vice, crime, ambition, injustice, oppression, slavery and war, proceed from their despising or neglecting the precepts contained in the Bible.[36]

What a strong statement! All the problems, unjust laws, and scandals in our present-day government—such as Whitewatergate, Travelgate, Filegate, Chinagate, and the "soap opera" sex scandals of Jennifer, Paula, and Monica-gate, stem from despising and neglecting the Word of God.

One last comment on Noah Webster. He truly passed on his godly heritage to his own children. William Webster, a son, authored a school textbook entitled *A Speller and Definer.* On the first page there is a picture of his father, Noah Webster, with this epigraph placed over it: "Who taught millions to read, but not one to sin."[37]

Before we discuss the last Christian educator, which will take us up to the 1960s, we need to look at an important turning point in American education. In 1892 the Kansas Teachers Union prepared a book for the commemoration of the 400th anniversary of Christopher Columbus Day. The Kansas Teachers Union made a decision to voluntarily turn elementary education over to the state. This decision was reluctantly made because of the increasing population. For over two and one-half centuries education had been nurtured in the lap of the church. The Kansas Teachers Union explained:

> Whether this [decision] was wise or not is not [our] purpose to discuss further than to remark, that if the study of the Bible is to be excluded from all state schools, if the inculcation of the principles of Christianity is to have no place in the daily program, if the worship of God is to form no part of the general exercises of these public elementary schools, then the good of the state would be better served by restoring all schools to church control.[38]

"Who taught millions to read, but not one to sin."

Portrait of Noah Webster, LL.D.

"Only two men have stood on the New World whose fame
is so sure to last, Columbus its discoverer, and Washington
its savior, Webster is and will be its great teacher; these
three make our trinity of fame."

It was made very clear by the Kansas Teachers Union that if the Bible, the principles of Christianity, and worship of God were removed from the public schools, the state should return all schools back to the church. Remember this statement was in 1892.

The last Christian educator we will examine was not only a great preacher, but an outstanding educator and president of Ohio University—Reverend William Holmes McGuffey, who earned the title "Schoolmaster of the Nation." He wrote the world-renowned textbooks, *McGuffey's Readers*. These readers are considered educational classics and were used in the public schools for over one hundred twenty-five years. The first *McGuffey's Reader* was authored in 1836. The second through the fourth readers were added later, along with two primers and a spelling textbook.

In the first seventy-five years, one hundred twenty-two million copies[39] of *McGuffey's Readers* were sold to schools and to the public. These readers taught biblical morality, character, and that God is Creator and Preserver. They also taught salvation through Jesus Christ, and a simple system of rewards and punishments. Up until the 1960s these readers were used by virtually every public school in America.

Let's review some of the lessons American boys and girls were taught from these readers.

Lesson 37 of the Eclectic First Reader was titled "Evening Prayer" and stressed the importance of daily communion with God.

Lesson 42 in this same reader was titled "Don't Take Strong Drink." It tells little boys and girls never to drink rum, whiskey, etc., unless they want to become drunkards. The Bible says no drunkard shall inherit the kingdom of heaven.

Lesson 21 of the Eclectic Third Reader was on "The Character of Jesus Christ."

The last lesson of the Eclectic Third Reader was the "Gospel Invitation," where boys and girls heard the "good news" about the Savior Jesus Christ.

Even up until this 1962 edition of *McGuffey's Readers,* the Old Deluder Satan Act, Dr. Benjamin Rush's *Defense of the Bible in School,* and the Northwest Ordinance, were listed and described in the foreword of the book. America truly does have a godly educational heritage. Up until the 1960s America's first schools, school laws, textbooks, even law books and hymnals, were based and centered on Christian principles and values from the Word of God. Our forefathers successfully passed on their godly heritage for almost three and one-half centuries.

Every aspect of life was touched in our American educational system. We call this a Christian worldview. It includes your personal beliefs about God, yourself, your neighbors, your family, civil government, national defense, art, music, history, morality, education, business, economics, and all other areas of life. This principle approach was a biblical education that primarily dealt with the inward man—in other words, forming character.

In the foreword of the 1962 *McGuffey's Reader* was a statement that related to the schoolroom and school books which would soon turn out to be America's worst nightmare come true:

> The world of the McGuffeys was a world where no one questioned the truths of the Bible or their relationships to everyday conduct, and where the notion that the separation of church and state required the exclusion of religion from the schoolroom or from school books seemed preposterous. The readers, therefore, are filled with stories from the Bible and tributes to its truth and beauty.

Sadly, in that same year, 1962, a radical turning point took place in America. The U.S. Supreme Court would hand down a ruling that would no longer permit prayer in the schools. In this case, *Engle vs. Vitale*,[40] the court—with a swipe of a pen—used the myth of separation of church and state to remove over three hundred twenty-five years of school prayer.

The phrase "separation of church and state" is not found anywhere in our U.S. Constitution, Bill of Rights, or Declaration of Independence, or congressional records. It *is* found in two other places. The first is Thomas Jefferson's personal letter[41] to the Danbury Baptist Church in Connecticut, in which he used this term to assure them that America would never have a national denomination running the country, as was the case in England. This was the same position and interpretation that our courts[42] and Congress[43] held for one hundred seventy years. However in 1962 the Supreme Court decided that "separation of church and state" would now mean any "religious activity" in public. The court had taken a brand-new direction which was unconstitutional and illegal. It was also one of the first court casts to attack Christianity in the public arena.

The second place where the phrase "separation of church and state" appears is in the former U.S.S.R. Constitution, in Appendix II, Document C, and Article 142.

Breach of laws governing the separation of church from state and of education from the church. Any breach of the laws governing the separation of the church from the state and of education from the church is punishable by corrective labor for a maximum term of one year or a fine of 50 rubles.

This makes it very clear that "separation of church and state" as defined by our courts since 1962 was not the original intent of our Founding Fathers, but was rather a communistic doctrine. Remember, the "evil empire" collapsed because of this tyrannical doctrine—and now America has instituted it.

Decades later, the myth of "separation of church and state" is still eating away and destroying our godly Christian heritage. In some cases student-led prayer before sporting events and prayer offered by the clergy at commencement ceremonies is now unconstitutional[44] and illegal. The latest onslaught on prayer is coming from Alabama's Judge Ira DeMent.

Christian parents, students, and lawyers in Alabama were aghast when Judge DeMent appointed a tax-funded monitor, Chris Doss, to enter classrooms to look for any teachers or students who would dare pray to God. Can you imagine this? In America? We now have secret "prayer police" in our schools making sure there are no prayers. This sounds like the Gestapo and the KGB.

In 1963 the U.S. Supreme Court made another unconstitutional, anti-Christian ruling. It struck down a law requiring the Holy Scriptures to be read in the public schools. In this case, *Abington vs. Schempp*,[45] over three hundred fifteen years of traditional Bible reading, reciting the Lord's Prayer, and using the Bible as a school textbook, were removed with the swipe of a pen.

One of the testimonies before the Supreme Court stated that "if portions of the New Testament were read without explanation, they could be and . . . had been psychologically harmful to the child." Can you believe that? If our school children read the Bible it could cause brain damage. Due to this court ruling, as well as the 1962 ruling, thirty-nine million students and over two million teachers could no longer read the Bible and pray together in the classroom. These activities are now totally censored. The myth of "separation of church and state" had now won two major victories for the revisionists and the secular humanists.

What would our Founding Fathers do if they were to come

Appendix II

Document C: *Articles of the Penal Code imposing penalties for religious crimes*

Art. 142. *Breach of laws governing the separation of Church from State and of Education from the Church.*

Any breach of laws governing the separation of the Church from the State and of Education from the Church is punishable by corrective labour for a maximum term of one year or a find of 50 roubles.[1]

Art. 143. *Interference with the celebration of religious rites.*

Anyone hindering the celebration of religious rites which do not disturb the public order or interfere with the rights of citizens, is liable to corrective labour for a maximum period of six months or to public censure.[2]

Art. 227. *Interference with the rights of citizens under cover of religious rites.*

The organization or leadership of a group whose activity, carried on under cover of preaching religious doctrines or celebrating religious rites, is prejudicial to the health, persons or rights of citizens, or incites them to refuse to take part in all social activities or to perform their civic duties, as also the enrollment of children in such a group, is punishable by deprivation of liberty for a maximum term of five years or by exile for the same term, with or without confiscation of property.

Active participation in the activities of such a group, as well as systematic incitement to the acts mentioned above, are punishable by deprivation of liberty for a maximum term of three years or by corrective labour for a maximum term of one year.

If the activities mentioned in the second paragraph of the present article, or the persons who engage in them, do not represent a serious social danger, social pressure can be brought to bear on them.[3]

(The first part of the corresponding article in the Penal Code of the Ukraine is slightly different in its formulation and carries heavier penalties.[4]).

[1] This article adopted on 8 December 1960 replaces Articles 122–6 of the former Code.

[2] Article 127 of the former Code (lighter penalty).

[3] Article adopted on 25 July 1962 and published in *Vedomosti Verkhovnogo Sovieta RSFSR* (Official Journal) 29, 1962.

[4] Article adopted on 27 July 1961 and published in *Vedomosti Verkhovnogo Sovieta Ukrainskoy SSR* 28, 1961

back and see that the Bible they had printed and put into schools—by an act of Congress—was now banned from being read in the classroom? They would all have spiritual heart attacks.

Amazingly enough, our schools are now filled with immorality, moral perversion, violence, hatred, and abuse—but no longer can the Bible be read to students. What a travesty! Not only is the Bible banned from being read in the classrooms, all the school textbooks that have been discussed would be banned. No more *New England Primers, Blue-Backed Spellers, McGuffey's Readers,* or hundreds of other Christ-centered school textbooks. This is censorship in the extreme. Martin Luther said concerning Bible reading being removed from the schools:

> I am much afraid that schools will prove to be the great gates of hell unless they diligently labor in explaining the Holy Scriptures, engraving them in the hearts of youth. I advise no one to place his child where the scriptures do not reign paramount. Every institution in which men are not increasingly occupied with the Word of God must become corrupt.[47]

The next major moral blow to our American schools and Christian heritage came in 1980 in the Supreme Court case *Stone vs. Graham.* The Ten Commandments were ruled unconstitutional and were removed from the school classroom. The court explained:

> If the posted copies of the Ten Commandments are to have any effect at all, it will be to induce the school children to read, meditate upon, perhaps to venerate and obey the Commandments. [This] . . . is not a permissible . . . objective.[48]

It is hard to believe this decision by our Supreme Court. School children would no longer be allowed to see the Ten Commandments because they might obey them. Things like "do not kill," "do not steal," "do not lie," and "do not take the Lord's name in vain" would be unconstitutional. This is unbelievable!

The Ten Commandments have been replaced by metal detectors, bars on the windows, video cameras, armed guards, and ID-wearing students. Since teachers can no longer teach the difference between right and wrong or moral absolutes, we have children murdering children, along with little girls having babies. We wonder why. Because America has forgotten God. Psalm 9:17 states: "The wicked shall be turned into hell, and all the nations that forget God."

There is one more Supreme Court case out of many which helped unravel the moral fiber of America. In this case, *Edwards vs. Aquillard,*[49] creation science—which had been taught in the schools for centuries—was ruled unconstitutional. This infamous case was originally tried in 1925 during the Scopes Monkey Trial. The American Civil Liberties Union lost the case at that time, but they came back in 1987 and won. In *Edwards vs. Aquillard* the theory of evolution alone would now be taught in all American schools. Once again—with the swipe of a pen—children are being taught the Big Bang Theory and that man evolved from pond slime millions of years ago.

This is now called "academic freedom." Recall what our nation's law books taught students—that God created everything, including mankind, in the six days of creation, and any law that would contradict the Holy Scriptures was not valid.

Passing laws that permit teaching the theory of evolution, not allowing the Ten Commandments and Bible reading or prayer in the classrooms, does absolutely contradict the Holy Scriptures. So why doesn't someone do something to stop these unjust, unconstitutional, and illegal court rulings? We no longer use *Blackstone's Commentaries on Law.* Our law schools and courts stopped using them around the 1930s. To properly understand this sobering reversal of common law to what is now called "case law," we need to go back to the year 1870 and Harvard University.

At this time, a man by the name of Christopher Langdell[50] became dean of Harvard Law School. Langdell believed whole-heartedly in Charles Darwin's theory of evolution. He also believed that as man evolved, his laws must also evolve. Since Langdell decided that judges should guide the evolution of the Constitution, he introduced what is known as the case law method into Harvard Law School. Case law basically means judges would interpret the U.S. Constitution and Bill of Rights as they believed it should be interpreted, ignoring our Founding Fathers original intent. In case law, should the judge or judges not believe in God or the Bible, Christian principles or values would not be used. If judges did not believe abortion was murder of babies, they ruled accordingly. If judges did not believe homosexuality was wrong, they ruled accordingly. And so the list goes on. This new case law method would open a Pandora's Box.

Our Founding Fathers used common law to interpret the Constitution and Bill of Rights, which was simply biblical law applied. We learned this from *Blackstone's Commentaries on Law.*

This case law method caused such an uproar among the other law professors at Harvard that they all resigned. Langdell then filled those vacant positions with law professors who held to this method of case law. Finally, after the seeds of case law had been sown to law students for decades, the harvest of corruption would come in the 1930s. *Blackstone's Commentaries,* based on common law or biblical law, was discarded. Other colleges and universities would now follow Harvard's footsteps.

The first major decision the courts made using the case law method was in 1962, the removal of prayer from the schools. From this point on, the floodgates of case law were unleashed to unravel the moral fiber of America and silence the Christian majority.

What were the results of removing biblical principles and values from the public schools? To best understand and examine the results, let us use the biblical admonition in Matthew 7:17 and 20: "Even so every good tree bringeth forth good fruit; but a corrupt tree bringeth forth evil fruit. . . . Wherefore by their fruits ye shall know them." We will simply compare and examine the fruits of the public schools before 1962 and up until recent years.

There are many good Christian teachers, principals, school board directors, and students in the public schools. Our battle is not against them, the revisionists, or the social engineers. Our battle, according to Ephesians 6:12, is "against principalities, against powers, against the rulers of darkness of this world, against spiritual wickedness in high places." We are truly in a spiritual battle and need to put on the whole armor of God.

The following charts are from David Barton of Wallbuilders. He uses government statistics to show that in 1962—the year religious principles and values were first separated from public affairs—was the year that started our schools down the infamous slippery slope to the dumbing down of American education.

The first chart shows SAT scores.[51] Up until 1963 SAT scores were very high and stayed within a ten point range. Then in 1963 the scores plummeted for almost two decades. An upturn began in 1981 with an explosion of private Christian schools and home-schooling. However, when attendance in those schools began to fall, the SAT scores took a nose dive once again.

Recall, we now have seventy-two million American adults that are functionally illiterate and another twenty-six million who cannot read or write at all. Many graduates cannot read their own diploma after twelve years of schooling!

SAT Total Scores

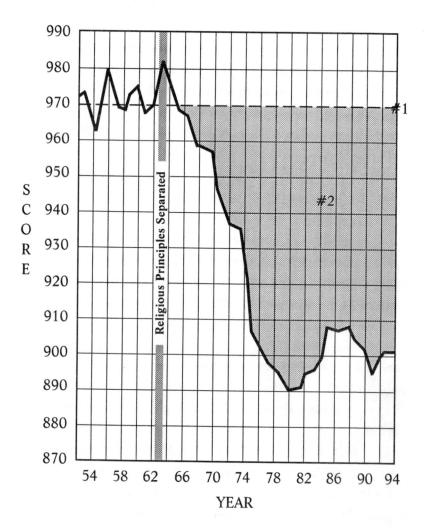

#1—Average achievement level prior to the separation
#2—Amount of reduced academic achievement since the separation

—Basic data from the College Entrance Exam Board

- Twenty-five percent of the seniors tested in Dallas, Texas, could not identify the country that borders the United States on the south, which is Mexico.[52]

- One-third of college seniors in American History thought the Magna Carta (signed in A.D. 1215) was what the Pilgrims signed on the Mayflower in 1620. The Pilgrims signed the Mayflower Compact.[53]

- One-fifth thought the "shot heard 'round the world" was fired at Gettysburg. (It was fired in Lexington in 1775, not Gettysburg in 1863.)[54]

Recently American students from fourth to twelfth grades participated in the Third International Mathematics and Science study. This study involved forty-one nations and more than one-half million students.[55] The results: Advanced Physics—incredibly, the United States finished dead last out of sixteen nations; Advanced Mathematics—the United States scored fifteenth out of sixteen nations. What an embarrassment and dismal failure. We could give pages of this kind of information.

The chart on the following page shows "Birth Rates for Unwed Girls 15-19 Years of Age."[56] The rates are low before 1963 and then skyrocket afterward. Teenage pregnancies have increased four hundred percent since 1962–63. Each day 2,756 teenage girls become pregnant. In 1990 the cost to taxpayers for teen mothers on welfare was $21.6 billion.[57]

The following is a grim statistic of an unwed teenage girl from New Jersey. While attending the high school prom, she gave birth to her baby in a bathroom stall. She dropped the baby in the trash, where it suffocated to death. She returned to the dance floor, requesting that the disc jockey play her favorite song, "The Unforgiven," by heavy metal band Metallica.[58]

Birth Rates for Unwed Girls
15–19 Years of Age

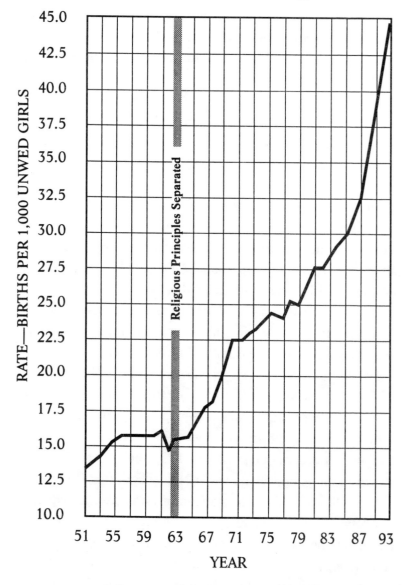

RATE—BIRTHS PER 1,000 UNWED GIRLS

Religious Principles Separated

YEAR

—Basic data from Department of Health and Human Services and
Statistical Abstracts of the United States

Recall that Founding Father Noah Webster taught millions of children to read and not one to sin. Now we have millions of children who are being taught to sin, but not taught to read.

The charts on the following pages show "Rape Arrests for Ages 13, 14, and 15." The charts start with 1965 as there were basically no problems prior to this year. For thirty years rape arrests have climbed to a point where it is not safe for young girls or women to be alone anywhere.

A survey[60] of seventeen hundred sixth through ninth grade students from eight cities was conducted by the Rhode Island Rape Crisis Center. This statement was given to the students: "It is okay for a man to force a woman to have sex against her consent if . . ."

. . . he has been dating her for six to twelve months. Sixty-five percent of the boys answered yes; forty-seven percent of the girls answered yes.

. . . he spends as much as ten to fifteen dollars on her. Twenty-four percent of the boys answered yes; sixteen percent of the girls answered yes.

. . . they are planning to get married. Seventy-four percent of the boys answered yes; sixty-seven percent of the girls answered yes.

What shocking and revealing attitudes of our youth.

Our government spends millions of our hard earned tax dollars for "safe sex" to be taught in schools. The following is a "safe sex" horror story. A fourteen-year-old girl in New York was raped in a public school classroom by three teenage classmates while a fourth classmate held her down. Two of the rapists stopped by the school counseling center to pick up con-

Rape Arrests: Ages 13–14

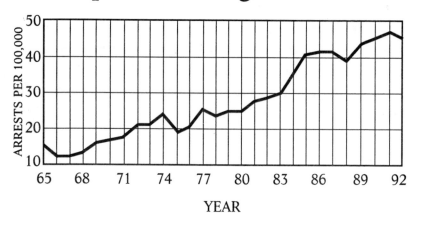

Rape Arrests: Age 15

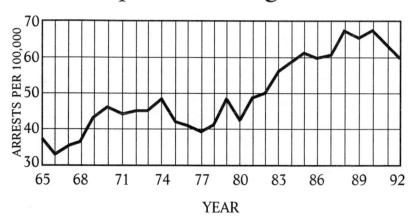

—Basic data from U.S. Department of Justice, FBI

doms prior to raping the girl.[61] So much for "safe sex"! God defined "safe sex" in His Word—one man with one woman until death do us part.

The next chart shows "Violent Behavior."[62] Prior to 1963 violence was at an all time low, and then an explosion took place after 1963. Recall that the top offenses in schools during the 1940s and 1950s were talking, chewing gum, and running in the hall. Today a few of the top offenses in our schools are murder, suicide, drug abuse, gang warfare, bombings, and the carrying of weapons.

The *Chicago Sun-Times* reported:

> A new security program that brought 150 police officers into the Chicago public schools resulted in an unprecedented 4,306 arrests [at school] in the first four months of this school year. . . . There were 1,122 arrests for disorderly conduct, 910 for battery, and 738 for criminal trespass . . . 229 [for] alleged weapons violations.[63]

Pay special attention to this next report:

> Bulletproof back-to-school clothes are the latest thing for children who run a dangerous gauntlet to and from class. School blazers and jackets are fitted with bullet resistant kevlar pads. Added shielding from flying bullets can be had from a bulletproof book bag or clipboard. They are offered by a former New York police officer.[64]

And there are more distressing statistics:

- 5,200 high school teachers are physically attacked each month, with one-fifth requiring medical treatment.[65]

Violent Behavior

Violent Crime: Number of Offenses

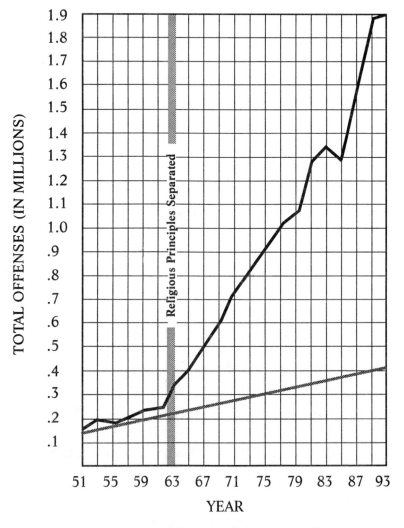

Indicates population growth profile

—Basic data from *Statistical Abstracts of the United States,*
and the Department of Commerce, Census Bureau

• The risk of violence to teenagers is greater in public schools than elsewhere.[66]

Do you know why God sent a worldwide flood in Noah's day? Genesis 6:11 and 13 tells us that it was because of violence.

The chart below shows "Murder Arrests: Ages 13-18."[67] The rate climbs rapidly from 1965, then levels off in the mid-1970s. In the 1980s—when the Ten Commandments were removed from the schools—the murder arrests once again sky-rocketed. Recently the nation was horrified and numbed at the spectacle of children killing children in our public schools. The following murder reports document that when a society begins to morally unravel, it is the youngest members who are most affected.

Jonesboro, Arkansas—Two young boys in Jonesboro, Ar-

Murder Arrests: Ages 13–18

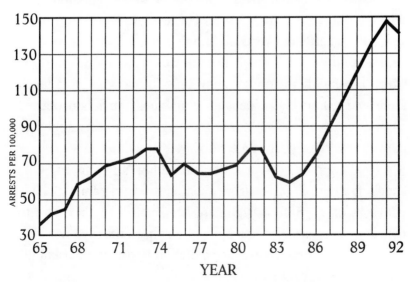

—Basic data from U.S. Department of Justice, FBI

kansas, ages 11 and 13, staged a schoolyard massacre against their classmates at Westside Middle School. The cousins had bedded down in the grass, waited for the fire alarm to empty the school, and then opened fire. When the smoke cleared four students and one teacher were dead, and eleven others wounded.[68]

Springfield, Oregon—Two months after the Jonesboro massacre, a fifteen-year-old boy in Springfield, Oregon, murdered both of his parents. He then went to school and mowed down his classmates in the cafeteria. When the shooting spree ended, one classmate was dead and nineteen others were wounded.[69]

Paducah, Kentucky—A few months earlier, a young boy opened fire on a student prayer meeting at Heath High School in Paducah, Kentucky, killing three classmates and wounding five more.[70]

Pearl, Mississippi—A few weeks earlier, a sixteen-year-old boy in Pearl, Mississippi, killed his mother. He then went to school and shot nine students, killing two, including his girlfriend.[71]

We need to ask ourselves a question: How can children commit these horrible crimes? John Hazlewood, whose fourteen-year-old son attends Westside Middle School in Jonesboro, Arkansas, said it best: "This is not the kids' problem, it's the way we're raising them today. They only know what you teach them."[72] The horrible incident at Columbine High School opened all of our eyes to the violence of teenagers, who seemingly are coping with the rigors of a school system without God.

What are many of our schools teaching our children? One shocking example comes from a tenth grade girl named Ashley, who tells of a writing assignment her English teacher gave to the class. The class had just studied Oedipus, the mythical king haunted by an oracle's tragic prediction that he would kill his father and marry his mother. Following is the teacher's assignment:

You're going to consult an oracle. It will tell you that you're going to kill your best friend. This is destined to happen, and there is absolutely no way out. You will commit this murder. What will you do before this event occurs? Describe how you felt leading up to it. How did you actually kill your best friend?[73]

Is it any wonder students are killing each other, killing their teachers and their parents after this type of emotional shock therapy? How did an assignment on how to kill your best friend get into the curriculum? To find out, we will be reviewing the excellent work of Mel and Norma Gabler, from Longview, Texas. They are truly watchdogs for children in the public schools. This couple has been evaluating school curriculums for over thirty-five year. This is what they found in the school textbooks in the 1970s and early 1980s.

A tenth grade English book has a poem which makes students think of suicide.

Razors pain you;
Rivers are damp;
Acids stain you;
And drugs cause cramp.
Guns aren't lawful;
Nooses give;
Gas smells awful;
You might as well live.[74]

After this poem, comments were given. "(A) Yeah, you might as well live; (B) suicide is a bit grim; (A), now if only I could think of a better way. . . ."

Another popular curriculum in many states is "Death Education." The following is found in a freshman level final exam:

"Prepare a booklet about your death. It must contain the following: death certificate, epitaph, funeral plan, and views on euthanasia."[75]

A high school psychology book stated: "A Hebrew legend tells how God created Adam by gathering dust from the four corners of the world."[76] Another chapter entitled "Sociological Functions of Myths" stated: "An excellent example is the Ten Commandments."[77] Another psychology book states that Jesus Christ's death and resurrection were also myths.[78] Can you believe your hard earned tax dollars are used to teach students that the Bible is full of myths?

God warns us in Colossians 2:8: "Beware lest any man spoil you through philosophy and vain deceit, after the tradition of men, after the rudiments of the world, and not after Christ." This verse simply means to stay away from false teaching that is devoid of truth. Ephesians 5:11 tells us: "And have no fellowship with the unfruitful works of darkness, but rather reprove them." This is exactly what we are doing—exposing the unfruitful works of darkness. We are truly in a spiritual battle and we need to put on the whole armor of God.

A sixth grade skills handbook explains to students a "witch license application."[79]

> Suppose that you wanted to pursue a career as a witch. These days you might have to apply for a license, and perhaps even join a witch's union. In any case, by filling out an application, your aptitude for witchcraft could be evaluated.

Questions in the application included: "What words would you use to cast a spell?" and "What is your favorite formula for a witches brew?" Many other school textbooks are so vulgar, vile, and wicked that they cannot be printed here. Remember, these school textbooks are from the 1970s and 1980s.

National Association of Witches (NAW)
(A Subsidiary of Sonic Brooms)
131313 Hades Highway
Satan's Corner, Lower Depths 02158

Witch license application

Professional name (do not give real name): _____

Business Address: _____

Age (as you wish to appear):_____ Phone number desired: _____

State why you wish to be a witch?

What animal impersonation do you prefer, and why?

What words would you use to cast a spell? (All incantation must be original.)

What is your favorite formula for a witches' brew? List ingredients in order used.

As a test of your ability to cast out spells, tell how you would handle the following problems:

1. A chicken that is normally cheerful and friendly takes to sulking in the corner of the henhouse.

2. A certain supermarket reports that all of its shopping carts seem to have trouble going in the right direction. A push forward sends them crashing sideways into the pickles.

3. A man in North Overshoe has brought suit against a local department store for selling him what he claims are faulty mirrors. He has purchased six mirrors to date and has returned them all because he claims that when he tries to shave in the morning the mirrors reflect the back of his head instead of his face.

_____
Signature of applicant

A high school homemaking book states: "Delbert and Sally are living together while they are in college. They do not expect to marry. They feel that living together provides each with love, affection, and support."[80] Our teenage children are being taught it is acceptable to commit fornication. But the Bible says in First Corinthians 6:9–10 "Be not deceived . . . fornicators . . . shall not inherit the kingdom of God."

The main source of sex education programs in public schools come from SIECUS, "Sex Information and Education Council of the United States." All of the sex education programs in our country are based in some part on research done at the Kinsey Institute, located at the University of Indiana in Bloomington. Alfred C. Kinsey founded this institute in 1948 and it is still in operation today. Medical experts, psychologists, and educators agree there is compelling evidence that the Kinsey Institute systematically molested and abused more than three hundred infants and children in their research.[81] Today that research forms the basis of sex education in the United States. To make matters worse, Kinsey was a homosexual, even though he was married and had three children.

Kinsey, who is largely credited with the sexual revolution, was also the father of child abuse. He lectured to thousands upon thousands of faculties and students on his university tours. This false evangelism of perverse theories and deviance beyond any imagination would have disastrous consequences for coming generations, starting in 1964. This is the year the Kinsey Institute launched SIECUS. Planned Parenthood was used as its field representatives to create a new sex education curriculum. Today these perverted sex education programs are usually presented to students under the guise of AIDS education and prevention. The programs were also adopted and approved by the Department of Education. Kinsey's perverse theories are promoted to our American children and teens. SIECUS receives approximately two hundred thousand dollars each year from our hard earned tax dollars, from the federal Centers for Disease Control, and from the Department of Health and Human Services.

After reviewing these school textbooks from the 1970s and 1980s, we can understand why students today are killing each other, committing suicide, involved in the occult, and have no moral absolutes. This leads us to another question.

How did all of this evil get into the textbooks in the first place? To properly understand, we must go back to the year 1837 and a man named Horace Mann, who was president of the Massachusetts state senate. Mann was a follower of Germany's new Hegelian philosophy, which claimed nothing was absolute and man's ideas were superior to biblical principles. Mann also favored the humanistic public schools which were then operating in the German state of Prussia. He was later able to push a few secular education laws through the Massachusetts legislature.

These few seeds of secular humanism were sown to the universities. In 1905 a group of five young men met in a loft above Peck's Restaurant at 140 Fulton Street in lower Manhattan. One of these men was the infamous Clarence Darrow. He would later be the lawyer for the American Civil Liberties Union in the Scope's Monkey Trial. Their plan was to overthrow the predominantly Christian worldview that still prevailed in America. They called their organization the Intercollegiate Socialist Society.[82] These men were ready to be exponents of an idea passed on to them by an obscure writer—Karl Marx. By using the proven method of gradualism taken from Roman general Quintus Fabius Maximus, they slowly infiltrated the public schools of our nation.

By 1912 there were chapters in forty-four colleges. By 1917 there were sixty-one chapters of student study groups in the

League of Industrial Democracy. At that time a man by the name of John Dewey, the godfather of progressive education, was the vice-president. By 1941 he had become president.

Dewey was a declared atheist who sometimes used religious terminology. He believed morals changed as society changed. Therefore, Dewey's theme was change and adjust, change and adjust. He was the first president of the American Humanist Association and a signer of Humanist Manifesto I in 1933.

What do secular humanists believe? According to Humanist Manifesto I and II:

- Religious humanists regard the universe as self-existing and not created.

- The human species is an emergence from natural evolutionary forces. . . .

- We reject all religious, ideological, or moral codes that . . . suppress freedom [or] dull intellect. . . .

- The right to birth control, abortion and divorce should be recognized.

- Individuals should be permitted to express their sexual . . . lifestyles as they desire.

- Promises of immortal salvation or fear of eternal damnation are both illusory and harmful. . . . There is no credible evidence that life survives the death of the body. . . .[83]

There is much, much more of this sort of devilish doctrine being taught to fifty-three million children in public schools. This statement was found in *Humanist* magazine (Jan./Feb. 1983).

This will send chills down the spine of every Bible believing Christian.

> ... The battle for mankind's future must be waged and won in the public school classroom by teachers who correctly perceive their role as the proselytizer of a new faith; a religion of humanity ... utilizing a classroom instead of a pulpit to convey humanist values in whatever subject they teach. .... The classroom must and will become an arena of conflict between the old and the new—the rotting corpse of Christianity, together with all its adjacent evils and misery and the new faith of humanism.[84]

Notice the agenda of humanism is to be taught in school classrooms in every subject. The U.S. Supreme Court ruled in *Torcaso vs. Watkin* that humanism is a religion, even though it does not teach or believe in the existence of God. Now that Christianity has been banned in the public schools, atheistic humanism is taught daily. This is the ultimate example of censorship.

The spread of humanism came from John Dewey to Dewey's disciples, who teach at teacher colleges. Teacher colleges graduate humanistic teachers, thus the educational establishment becomes humanistic. Public schools graduate students with humanistic philosophies. We have humanists in the media, education, government, and law. Who was—and is—the supporter and mover-and-shaker of this new radical educational system? Who influences more legislation, makes more policies, and elects more candidates than any government party? It's not the Democratic or Republican party.

The biggest supporter of John Dewey was—and still is—the National Education Association (NEA) located in Washington, D.C. In 1933 Dewey became its honorary president. The NEA today is the largest and most powerful union in the nation.

Its membership includes approximately 2.4 million teachers, administrators, and support personnel. These union members pay dues to the NEA, then much of the monies are spent for left-wing lobbying. The NEA is pro-abortion, pro-homosexual, anti-parent, and anti-home school. The NEA dictates what children are taught in school from sex, to AIDS, to globalism, to diversity (a code word for gay/lesbian preferences). The NEA supports the entire radical feminist agenda, including federal day-care and tax-funded abortions. NEA resolutions show no interest in teaching the four Rs: reading, writing, 'rithmetic, and right or wrong. Unfortunately, many Christians indirectly support this agenda through their union dues.

There is a way out of paying those dues. Christian teachers who do not want to violate their conscience can contact an organization called the National Right to Work Committee, located in Springfield, Virginia. There are many teachers who oppose the NEA's radical agenda. They picket the annual NEA meeting in Kansas City.

After the revisionists and social engineers had accomplished their dirty work in the school textbooks, they spent billions of our tax dollars for what is called "behavior modification"[86] in the mid-eighties. The purpose of this new teaching tool was to learn how to influence people, including children, to do things without their knowing they were being influenced. American children were now going to be used as human guinea pigs and rats, like in school laboratories. To deceive parents, sugar—coated words were used for subjects like values clarification, situation ethics, alternative lifestyles, and political correctness.

This assault on pupil and parental rights, along with the psychological abuse of children in the public school, finally came to a point in 1984, and official hearings were held by the U.S. Department of Education. Hundreds of parents traveled to one of seven locations to testify at these hearings, all of which are documented. Phyllis Schlafly, a constitution lawyer, author, and founder and president of Eagle Forum in Alton, Illinois, has printed the official transcripts of these proceedings in her national bestselling book, *Child Abuse in the Classroom.* This book should be required reading for every parent and taxpayer.

Child Abuse in the Classroom allows you to read with your own eyes concerning the hearings. It explains why we now have seventy-two million functionally illiterate adults who have graduated from public schools. These hearings explain why young people are experiencing high rates of teenage suicide, loneliness, premarital sex, pregnancies, and abortions; how children learn in schools to be sexually active, take illegal drugs, repudiate their parents, and rationalize immoral behavior when it feels good in a particular situation. These hearings speak with the thunderous voices of hundreds of angry parents. Their children have been emotionally, morally, and intellectually abused by psychological and behavioral experiments during classroom hours. The parents assumed their children were being taught basic knowledge and skills. Parents were outraged about their tax dollars being used for these hideous purposes. The results of these hearings on September 6, 1984, finally implemented the "Protection of Pupil Rights Amendment," also known as the "Hatch Amendment."

We applaud the hundreds of brave parents, the Hatch Amendment, and Eagle Forum, for all of their time and talent in striving to bring our public schools back to moral sanity.

Until the hearts of men and women are changed, laws and amendments will be broken and sidestepped, or slick lawyers will find loopholes. Jeremiah 17:9 states: "The heart is deceitful above all things and desperately wicked; who can know it?" America needs a spiritual heart change, not more laws, government, and money to fix the problems.

As we moved into the 1990s, everyone hoped for education

to improve. Once again, the statistics show even more "behavior modification" and "dumbing down" of children in the public schools. To better understand why this is happening, consider the following shocking statement by Harvard professor Chester M. Pierce, which was made to two thousand teachers in Denver, Colorado:

> Every child in America entering school at the age of five is insane because he comes to school with certain allegiances towards our founding fathers, toward his parents, toward a belief in a supernatural being. . . . It is up to you teachers to make all of these sick children well by creating the international children of the future.[87]

It is clear to see from this statement that teachers will be the architect for creating the New World Order.

There is one radical behavior modification agenda being implemented and promoted in many public schools which God will not tolerate much longer. As a matter of fact, God made an example and judged this sinful and wicked agenda in Genesis 19. He then stated in Second Peter 2:6 that the same judgement would be given to those that would later commit this ungodly sin. If you recall, our nations first law books, *Blackstone's Commentaries on Law,* stated that it was a disgrace to even mention this sin. Sadly, this sin is no longer called sin; it is instead called "gay rights." God destroyed two cities for committing homosexuality. He made them examples to all future generations so that they would not be destroyed as well. We need to become better informed on the radical gay rights agenda in the schools. The destruction of the precious young lives and health of all our American children are hanging in the balance. You must become better informed, so put on your spiritual safety belts.

Recall, America's first textbook, the *New England Primer,* taught the ABCs using Bible verses. According to the *Washington Times,*[88] preschoolers in Provincetown, Massachusetts, are being taught the ABCs of being gay. First graders in California have a new curriculum entitled "Gay-Ed for Tots."[89] In New York the curriculum entitled "Children of the Rainbow"[90] includes books like *Daddy's Roommate, Heather Has Two Mommies,* and *Gloria Goes to Gay Pride.* Once again, this is being taught to first graders. A poster[91] with a phone number hangs in a Los Angeles school encouraging children to contact homosexual and lesbian recruiters.

America's first school, Harvard, graduated preachers and missionaries. Now, Harvard's United Ministry has announced that the University Memorial Church will begin hosting same-sex union ceremonies, preformed by "Reverend" Peter Gomes,[92] an openly homosexual leader. Harvard, along with Princeton, Yale, and many other universities across America, now celebrate and promote Gay and Lesbian Awareness Day. We have surely come a long way—in the wrong direction.

Parents, please check your children's textbooks for information on homosexual lifestyles. Go to your PTA meetings. Ask your children's teachers if they teach any subjects on alternative lifestyles. *Your child could be the next victim.*

Another way to become informed on the new radical curriculum is by reading a book entitled *Brave New Schools*[93] by Berit Kjos. She is a concerned parent, a widely respected researcher, columnist, and conference speaker. Some of the information in *Brave New Schools* documents how sorcery, the occult, divination, altered states of consciousness, death education, sacred sex, and global spirituality are being taught in the schools. Just a few (out of many) programs about which you as a parent need to be aware are: Pumsy the Dragon, Quest, Mission SOAR, Impressions, Guided Imagery, Mind Mapping, Visualization, Med-

NEED TO TALK?
CALL THE
GAY & LESBIAN
YOUTH TALKLINE

THE LINE IS STAFFED BY TRAINED VOLUNTEERS WHO WILL HELP YOU ACCESS THE GAY & LESBIAN COMMUNITY, AND EXPLORE YOUR FEELINGS & THOUGHTS IN A SAFE, ANNONYMOUS MANNER. THE TALKLINE ALSO PROVIDES AIDS INFORMATION; & REFERRAL TO YOUTH

THE LINE IS IN OPERATION

7:00 pm until 10:00 pm (Thursdays)   7:00 pm until Midnight (Fridays & Saturdays)

(213) 462-8130

A SERVICE OF THE TRIANGOS YOUTH OUTREACH PROGRAM OF THE
GAY & LESBIAN COMMUNITY SERVICES CENTER LOS ANGELES.

icine Wheel, and SCAMS. Other programs teach world government, world citizenship, world religion, and a global economy. Many of these programs are documented and explained in *Brave New Schools*.

Where is the radical education system taking us? What is going to happen to our children and our nation? Our children are being prepared to be "worker bees" in the new global economy of the New World Order. Let me explain and document this statement from a letter written to Hillary Rodham Clinton in 1992. This eighteen-page letter is from the National Center on Education and the Economy (NCEE), located in Washington, D.C. It is addressed to:

Hillary Clinton
The Governor's Mansion
1800 Canter Street
Little Rock, Arkansas 72206

Members of the Board of Trustees of the NCEE include:

- Honorary chair—Mario Cuomo
- Chairman—John Sculley, then president and CEO of Apple computer
- President—Mark Tucker
- Hillary R. Clinton, the key person in all of this
- Ira Magaziner, who was the engineer of the 1993 plan to socialize health care
- David Rockefeller, Jr., a mover and shaker of the New World Order

This letter is dated November 11, 1992, and is from Mark Tucker. (The complete text of this letter is included as an appendix beginning on page 91.) Remember, this is 1992, right after Bill

Clinton won the presidential election. The letter begins:

> Dear Hillary:
>
> I still cannot believe you won. . . . I met last Wednesday in David Rockefeller's office with him and John Sculley. . . . It was a great celebration. Both John and David were more expansive than I have ever seen them. . . . The subject we were discussing was what you and Bill should do about combining education, training, and labor market policy.

Combining education and labor is one of the first principles of the Marxist–Leninist theory of communistic education . . .
Mark Tucker continues:

> There is a great opportunity and the country's last chance to remold the entire American educational system through legislation and enacted as a program. This is the plan of least resistance. . . .

A little further down in the letter Mr. Tucker describes his vision for "human resource" development plan as a "seamless web" that "literally extends from the cradle to the grave for everyone young and old, poor and rich, worker and full time student." Another word for all of this is "socialism." Incidentally, human resource is a Marxist term coined by Hegel in the 1850s.

This letter from the National Center on Education and the Economy outlines the plan for the government to take over the educational system—lock, stock, and barrel.

In a report co-chaired by Hillary Clinton and Ira Magaziner, the NCEE stated: "By the year 2000 over seventy percent of the jobs in America will not require a college education."[94] Within a week of the 1992 presidential elections Hillary Clinton was reading the NCEE eighteen-page letter, which recommended to "remodel the entire American educational system." The letter also recommended a national "employment service" to match job seekers with job providers and a "new system of labor market boards."[95] To control all education, jobs, and job training—period. Instead of being individual self-directed souls with exciting, unpredictable potential, children would now become "human resources" in a planned global economy.

We can see by these statements from the NCEE that students are being prepared to be worker bees in the global economy of the New World Order.

This radical agenda by the NCEE and Hillary and Bill Clinton was implemented in two crucial pieces of legislation which were made law in 1994. The first was the Goals 2000 Educate America Act and the second was the School-to-Work Opportunities Act.

The first law, "Goals 2000," contains ten titles and one hundred fifty-five pages of complex legislation. This system has little to do with academics. It is the centerpiece to restructure and reform our schools according to the federal government agenda, which is a New World Order.

In a nutshell Goals 2000 has three common themes: global government, global economy, and global spirituality, which is in reality New Age paganism. These three global themes are well documented in an excellent book by Kathy Finnegan entitled *Goals 2000: Restructuring Our School—Restructuring Our Society.*[96] This three hundred fifty-page book takes the reader through all ten titles of Goals 2000 and exposes this radical agenda in laymen terms.

Two sinister aspects (out of many) in Goals 2000 about which we need to be informed and aware are "National Information Infrastructure" and "Portable Credentials."

The "National Information Infrastructure"[97] is described in

Title 2, Section I, and will set up a national data bank. This will keep track of all children from birth (when they receive a Social Security number) through schooling, employment, retirement, and death. This unconstitutional tracking and numbering of U.S. citizens from the cradle to the grave is only one example of the government's intrusion into the lives of your children. This infrastructure reminds you of the system set up by the Antichrist in Revelation 13 where "no man might buy or sell unless he had . . . the number of the beast."

"Portable Credentials" are described in Title 5, Section D, and will determine "employment security." We will see shortly that this could very well mean the government will ultimately decide if and where a student will go to college, where they will live, where they will work, and for how long. Once again, there will be "lifelong" monitoring by the state. United States citizens could soon be hearing the same words spoken by the KGB: "Show me your papers."

Let's look at the second law, the "School-to-Work Opportunities Act." This law formed a partnership between the U.S. Departments of Education and Labor. Recall this is the first principle in the Marxist–Leninist theory of communistic education. The pilot state to use School-to-Work and Goals 2000 was Oregon. It was then to be instituted nationwide.

On June 16, 1994, Connie Chung's "Eye on America" camera crew focused on high school sophomores who were parading across Oregon's Cottage Grove High School stage. Students who proved they passed an outcome-based education test were handed a Certificate of Initial Mastery.[99] This certificate is not to be confused with the traditional diploma. Mark Tucker of the NCEE created the Certificate of Initial Mastery.

That same day, many parents and students were caught on film by CBS-TV protesting this certificate. One high school sophomore, Nicole Doggett, stated: "Frankly, I find it difficult to be

Certificate of Initial Mastery

Cottage Grove High School by authority of the Oregon State
Department of Education and the South Lane School District

presents this certificate to

Jay Terrison

In recognition of meeting standards for the Certificate of Initial
Mastery.

_____
June 16, 1994
Date

Involved Citizen
Quality Producer
Self-Directed Learner
Constructive Thinker
Effective Communicator
Collaborative Contributor

Quantify
Apply Math/Science
Understand Diversity
Deliberate on Public Issues
Interpret Human Experience
Understand Positive Health Habits

_____
Steve Pirsley
Superintendent

_____
Ed Otto
Principal

_____
Mary Gabriel Adams
Lead Teacher

proud of this piece of paper, because I did not receive the education I deserved."[100] Interestingly, out of the two hundred ninety-nine students who started this program, there were one hundred seventy-five left after two years, and only seventy-four of those students received the Certificate of Initial Mastery.

Under the original language of School-to-Work, a student would not be able to graduate, attend college, or be employed without a Certificate of Initial Mastery. In other words, students would be required to meet all of the federal government's politically correct goals from A to Z. As a matter of fact, the NCEE stated: "Those without a Certificate of Initial Mastery will be condemned to dead end jobs that would leave them in poverty even if they are working."[101] Thanks to concerned parents in the final passage of School-to-Work, the language was removed that required students to have the Certificate of Initial Mastery. The framework still remains to be made law by administrative ruling without legislative oversight.

In the year 2002 the Oregon Education Act for the twenty-first century will require all students to earn the Certificate of Initial Mastery as a prerequisite to enroll in a college or university. It is easy to see that our government is gradually weaving its seamless web of tyrannical usurpations over all of us.

School-to-Work failed in the former U.S.S.R., Germany, China, Japan, England, Switzerland, the Netherlands, and Cuba. Amazingly forty-eight of the United States of America have now initiated this Marxist–Leninist principle. They have combined schooling with productive labor, repackaged it, and call it School-to-Work. We are now going down the same slippery slope that has failed worldwide. Many teachers and parents are not even aware of what is happening to their students and children.

For centuries parents have been the consumer of public schools, but now under School-to-Work parents are the suppliers. They will now supply the children, which is the product or human resource, to the schools, who will in turn shape the product, which is the child, for the specifications of the new consumer, which is business and industry. This new philosophy is called Total Quality Management—TQM.

The federal government will keep track of all students by a system called "Worklink."[102] It will then decide where each student will work in the new global economy. Twenty percent might be food handlers, ten percent might be plumbers and electricians, fifty percent might be common laborers, five percent might be doctors. This radical restructuring has truly been a well orchestrated takeover of American children and the public education system. Is it now clear that students are being prepared to be worker bees in the New World Order?

Next, we will see how the United Nations will be a key player in global education. In 1975 an essay entitled "The Need for Global Education"[103] was published. It was distributed by UNESCO, a United Nations organization. This essay was authored by Robert Muller, who at the time was the United Nations secretary general (he was called the "prophet of hope"). Muller has been a recognized leader in the occult New Age movement for at least three decades.

One of the New Age organizations that he endorses is the World Constitution and Parliament Association, located in Lakewood, Colorado.[104] There are over fifteen million members from eighty countries. The World Constitution is now being circulated worldwide for ratification by the nations and people of earth. The preamble reads like something out of a New Age occult manual:

> Realizing that humanity today has come to a turning point in history and that we are on the threshold of a New World Order which promises to usher in an era of peace, prosperity, justice, and harmony.[105]

Did you hear the buzz words "New World Order" and "peace"? This World Constitution not only calls for a world government, but a world economy, world religion, world police, and naturally a Department of World Education. Here is Robert Muller's endorsement of the World Constitution:

> I support wholeheartedly the brilliant and modern World Constitution and Parliament Association. It is here at the right moment when the world needs salvation from its present chaos and a metamorphosis into a new appropriate world order to cope with the massive global problems confronting us. May God bless this Constitution, signed Robert Muller.[104]

This statement sounds like a paraphrase of Revelation 13 where the Antichrist will set up a world government.

Because of the worldwide outcry for global education, Muller drafted the World Core Curriculum.[107] This was formally introduced in his 1984 book, *New Genesis—Shaping a Global Spirituality.* The World Core Curriculum set forth the principles for global education. Amazingly many teachers, administrators, and Christians are not aware that this important document exists.

The World Core Curriculum is now being used in Goals 2000 in Eugene, Oregon's elementary schools, grades K thru five.[108] In the preface of the World Core Curriculum we find that this work by Robert Muller originated from the ageless wisdom of the teachings set forth in the books of Alice Bailey.

Alice Bailey was a renowned occultist and was called the mother of the New Age movement. Alice Bailey wrote twenty-four occult books, and in 1921 founded the Lucifer Publishing Company.[109] A short time later she changed the name from Lucifer Publishing Company to Lucis Trust, which until a few years ago was headquartered at the United Nations Plaza in New York City.[110]

THE CONSCIOUSNESS OF THE ATOM

by

ALICE A. BAILEY

a series of lectures delivered in New York City
Winter of 1921–22

Author of
"Letters on Occult Meditation"
"Initiation, Human and Solar"

First Edition

Lucifer Publishing Co.
135 Broadway
New York City.

Alice Bailey stated that her teacher was a Tibetan teacher, Djwhal Khul.[111] Djwhal Khul never existed, at least not as a real person. You see, Djwhal Khul was Alice Bailey's spirit guide. She was a channeler. According to Deuteronomy 18, in reality Alice Bailey contacted or channeled a demon spirit.

So the United Nations World Core Curriculum document designed to chart the future course of public education worldwide (including Goals 2000) was based upon the teachings of an occultist and a demon. Pretty unbelievable, isn't it? The students are now being taught doctrines of demons, and most parents have no clue what is happening.

If they were ever going to succeed in ushering in the worldwide reign of their christ, who is really the Antichrist spoken of in Revelation 13, the schools would need to be brought under the direct control of Luciferic occultists.

I trust you now understand how and why American students have been transformed "from Harvard scholars to worker bees of the New World Order."

What should we as Christians do?

One, we need to become informed and know biblical truth. Hosea 4:6 states: "My people are destroyed for a lack of knowledge. . . ."

Two, get involved. We are to be salt and light in our sphere of influence, which includes public education. As the Lord leads, get involved and attend PTA meetings, learn what your school board directors believe, consider running for a school board position, review school textbooks, and network with other concerned Christian parents and organizations. Vote for godly men and women who have proven track records. Write and call your congressmen concerning laws that infringe on our God-given rights and freedoms. Write letters to the editor. Call in and speak out on radio talk programs. Give this book to your family, friends, church, neighbors, and public officers.

Three, do not be fearful. Second Timothy 1:7 states: "For God hath not given us the spirit of fear; but of power, and of love, and of a sound mind."

Four, unless your public school is an exception and teaches biblical principles, values, and academics, enroll your children in alternative schooling, namely home schooling or a carefully screened private Christian school. God will provide a way if you trust Him and pray.

Five, pray for a heaven-sent revival according to the principles in Second Chronicles 7:14: "If my people, which are called by my name, shall humble themselves, and pray, and seek my face, and turn from their wicked ways; then will I hear from heaven, and will forgive their sin, and will heal their land." Remember this verse is speaking to God's people. We will not have revival in the schoolhouse or the White House until we first have revival in the church house.

Last, but most important, be a soul winner. Proverbs 11:30 states: "He that winneth souls is wise." Give the gospel to teachers, school leaders, students, and government officials. You cannot change a person's mind until Jesus Christ changes their heart.

Speaking of souls, maybe some of you do not know for sure if all of your sins are forgiven. If you died in the next few minutes, would you go to heaven?

Recall the *New England Primer* and how the boys and girls learned the ABCs with Bible verses. "E" stood for: "Except a man be born again he cannot see the kingdom of God." All of us have been born into this world physically, but everyone must be born a second time from above, a spiritual birth which takes place in a person's heart. This is done by asking Jesus Christ, who died on the cross for your sins, was buried, and rose again, to come into your life and forgive you of all your sins. This is also called repentance, which means a change of mind. Jesus said, "Except ye repent, ye shall all likewise perish."

The letter "N" stood for: "Now is the accepted time, now is the day of salvation." Now is the time to give your life to Jesus Christ. Don't wait another minute. Tomorrow may be too late.

The letter "L" stood for: "Liars shall have their part in the lake which burns with fire and brimstone." Every person who rejects God's only begotten Son, Jesus Christ, will one day have to pay for their own sins in a terrible place called the lake of fire. *Please receive Jesus Christ's gift of eternal life today.*

The Northwest Ordinance

An Ordinance for the government of the Territory of the United States northwest of the River Ohio.

Be it ordained by the United States in Congress assembled, That the said territory, for the purposes of temporary government, be one district, subject, however, to be divided into two districts, as future circumstances may, in the opinion of Congress, make it expedient.

Be it ordained by the authority aforesaid, That the estates, both of resident and nonresident proprietors in the said territory, dying intestate, shall descent to, and be distributed among their children, and the descendants of a deceased child, in equal parts; the descendants of a deceased child or grandchild to take the share of their deceased parent in equal parts among them: And where there shall be no children or descendants, then in equal parts to the next of kin in equal degree; and among collaterals, the children of a deceased brother or sister of the intestate shall have, in equal parts among them, their deceased parents' share; and there shall in no case be a distinction between kindred of the whole and half blood; saving, in all cases, to the widow of the intestate her third part of the real estate for life, and one third part of the personal estate; and this law relative to descents and dower, shall remain in full force until altered by the legislature of the district. And until the governor and judges shall adopt laws as hereinafter mentioned, estates in the said territory may be devised or bequeathed by wills in writing, signed and sealed by him or her in whom the estate may be (being of full age), and attested by three witnesses; and real estates may be conveyed by lease and release, or bargain and sale, signed, sealed and delivered by the person being of full age, in whom the estate may be, and attested by two witnesses, provided such wills be duly proved, and such conveyances be acknowledged, or the execution thereof duly proved, and be recorded within one year after proper magistrates, courts, and registers shall be appointed for that purpose; and personal property may be transferred by delivery; saving, however to the French and Canadian inhabitants, and other settlers of the Kaskaskies, St. Vincents and the neighboring villages who have heretofore professed themselves citizens of Virginia, their laws and customs now in force among them, relative to the descent and conveyance, of property.

Be it ordained by the authority aforesaid, That there shall be appointed from time to time by Congress, a governor, whose commission shall continue in force for the term of three years, unless sooner revoked by Congress; he shall reside in the district, and have a freehold estate therein in 1,000 acres of land, while in the exercise of his office.

There shall be appointed from time to time by Congress, a secretary, whose commission shall continue in force for four years unless sooner revoked; he shall reside in the district, and have a freehold estate therein in 500 acres of land, while in the exercise of his office. It shall be his duty to keep and preserve the acts and laws passed by the legislature, and the public records of the district, and the proceedings of the governor in his executive department, and transmit authentic copies of such acts and proceedings, every six months, to the Secretary of Congress: There shall also be appointed a court to consist of three judges, any two of whom to form a court, who shall have a common law jurisdiction, and reside in the district, and have each therein a freehold estate in 500 acres of land while in the exercise of their offices; and their commissions shall continue in force during good behavior.

The governor and judges, or a majority of them, shall adopt and publish in the district such laws of the original States, criminal and civil, as may be necessary and best suited to the circumstances of the district, and report them to Congress from time to time: which laws shall be in force in the district until the organization of the General Assembly therein, unless disapproved of by Congress; but afterwards the Legislature shall have authority to alter them as they shall think fit.

The governor, for the time being, shall be commander in chief of the militia, appoint and commission all officers in the same below the rank of general officers; all general officers shall be appointed and commissioned by Congress.

Previous to the organization of the general assembly, the governor shall appoint such magistrates and other civil officers in each county or township, as he shall find necessary for the preservation of the peace and good order in the same: After the general assembly shall be organized, the powers and duties of the magistrates and other civil officers shall be regulated and defined by the said assembly; but all magistrates and other civil officers not herein otherwise directed, shall during the continuance of this temporary government, be appointed by the governor.

For the prevention of crimes and injuries, the laws to be adopted or made shall have force in all parts of the district, and for the execution of process, criminal and civil, the governor shall make proper divisions thereof; and he shall proceed from time to time as circumstances may require, to lay out the parts of the district in which the Indian titles shall have been extinguished, into counties and townships, subject, however, to such alterations as may thereafter be made by the legislature.

So soon as there shall be five thousand free male inhabitants of full age in the district, upon giving proof thereof to the governor, they shall receive authority, with time and place, to elect a representative from their counties or townships to represent them in the general assembly: Provided, That, for every five hundred free male inhabitants, there shall be one representative, and so on progressively with the number of free male inhabitants shall the right of representation increase, until the number of representatives shall amount to twenty five; after which, the number and proportion of representatives shall be regulated by the legislature: Provided, That no person be eligible or qualified to act as a representative unless he shall have been a citizen of one of the United States three years, and be a resident in the district, or unless he shall have resided in the district three years; and, in either case, shall likewise hold in his own right, in fee simple, two hundred acres of land within the same; Provided, also, That a freehold in fifty acres of land in the district, having been a citizen of one of the states, and being resident in the district, or the like freehold and two years residence in the district, shall be necessary to qualify a man as an elector of a representative.

The representatives thus elected, shall serve for the term of two years; and, in case of the death of a representative, or removal from office, the governor shall issue a writ to the county or township for which he was a member, to elect another in his stead, to serve for the residue of the term.

The general assembly or legislature shall consist of the governor, legislative council, and a house of representatives. The Legislative Council shall consist of five members, to continue in office five years, unless sooner removed by Congress; any three of whom to be a quorum: and the members of the Council shall be nominated and appointed in the following manner, to wit: As soon as representatives shall be elected, the Governor shall appoint a time and place for them to meet together; and, when met, they shall nominate ten persons, residents in the district, and each possessed of a freehold in five hundred acres of land, and return their names to Congress; five of whom Congress shall appoint and commission to serve as aforesaid; and, whenever a vacancy shall happen in the council, by death or removal from office, the house of representatives shall nominate two persons, qualified as aforesaid, for each vacancy, and return their names to Congress; one of whom congress shall appoint and commission for the residue of the term. And every five years, four months at least before the expiration of the time of service of the members of council, the said house shall nominate ten persons, qualified as aforesaid, and return their names to Congress; five of whom Congress shall appoint and commission to serve as members of the council five years, unless sooner removed. And the governor, legislative council, and house of representatives, shall have authority to make laws in all cases, for the good government of the district, not repugnant to the principles and articles in this ordinance established and declared. And all bills, having passed by a majority in the house, and by a majority in the council, shall be referred to the governor for his assent; but no bill, or legislative act whatever, shall be of any force without his assent. The governor shall have power to convene, prorogue, and dissolve the general assembly, when, in his opinion, it shall be expedient.

The governor, judges, legislative council, secretary, and such other officers as Congress shall appoint in the district, shall take an oath or affirmation of fidelity and of office; the governor before the president of congress, and all other officers before the Governor. As soon as a legislature shall be formed in the district, the council and house assembled in one room, shall have authority, by joint ballot, to elect a delegate to Congress, who shall have a seat in Congress, with a right of debating but not voting during this temporary government.

And, for extending the fundamental principles of civil and

religious liberty, which form the basis whereon these republics, their laws and constitutions are erected; to fix and establish those principles as the basis of all laws, constitutions, and governments, which forever hereafter shall be formed in the said territory: to provide also for the establishment of States, and permanent government therein, and for their admission to a share in the federal councils on an equal footing with the original States, at as early periods as may be consistent with the general interest:

It is hereby ordained and declared by the authority aforesaid, That the following articles shall be considered as articles of compact between the original States and the people and States in the said territory and forever remain unalterable, unless by common consent, to wit:

Article I.

No person, demeaning himself in a peaceable and orderly manner, shall ever be molested on account of his mode of worship or religious sentiments, in the said territory.

Article II.

The inhabitants of the said territory shall always be entitled to the benefits of the writ of habeas corpus, and of the trial by jury; of a proportionate representation of the people in the legislature; and of judicial proceedings according to the course of the common law. All persons shall be bailable, unless for capital offenses, where the proof shall be evident or the presumption great. All fines shall be moderate; and no cruel or unusual punishments shall be inflicted. No man shall be deprived of his liberty or property, but by the judgment of his peers or the law of the land; and, should the public exigencies make it necessary, for the common preservation, to take any person's property, or to demand his particular services, full compensation shall be made for the same. And, in the just preservation of rights and property, it is understood and declared, that no law ought ever to be made, or have force in the said territory, that shall, in any manner whatever, interfere with or affect private contracts or engagements, bona fide, and without fraud, previously formed.

Article III.

Religion, morality, and knowledge, being necessary to good government and the happiness of mankind, schools and the means of education shall forever be encouraged. The utmost good faith shall always be observed towards the Indians; their lands and property shall never be taken from them without their consent; and, in their property, rights, and liberty, they shall never be invaded or disturbed, unless in just and lawful wars authorized by Congress; but laws founded in justice and humanity, shall from time to time be made for preventing wrongs being done to them, and for preserving peace and friendship with them.

Article IV.

The said territory, and the States which may be formed therein, shall forever remain a part of this Confederacy of the United States of America, subject to the Articles of Confederation, and to such alterations therein as shall be constitutionally made; and to all the acts and ordinances of the United States in Congress assembled, conformable thereto. The inhabitants and settlers in the said territory shall be subject to pay a part of the federal debts contracted or to be contracted, and a proportional part of the expenses of government, to be apportioned on them by Congress according to the same common rule and measure by which apportionments thereof shall be made on the other States; and the taxes for paying their proportion shall be laid and levied by the authority and direction of the legislatures of the district or districts, or new States, as in the original States, within the time agreed upon by the United States in Congress assembled. The legislatures of those districts or new States, shall never interfere with the primary disposal of the soil by the United States in

Congress assembled, nor with any regulations Congress may find necessary for securing the title in such soil to the bona fide purchasers. No tax shall be imposed on lands the property of the United States; and, in no case, shall nonresident proprietors be taxed higher than residents. The navigable waters leading into the Mississippi and St. Lawrence, and the carrying places between the same, shall be common highways and forever free, as well to the inhabitants of the said territory as to the citizens of the United States, and those of any other States that may be admitted into the confederacy, without any tax, impost, or duty therefore.

Article V.

There shall be formed in the said territory, not less than three nor more than five States; and the boundaries of the States, as soon as Virginia shall alter her act of cession, and consent to the same, shall become fixed and established as follows, to wit: The western State in the said territory, shall be bounded by the Mississippi, the Ohio, and Wabash Rivers; a direct line drawn from the Wabash and Post Vincents, due North, to the territorial line between the United States and Canada; and, by the said territorial line, to the Lake of the Woods and Mississippi. The middle State shall be bounded by the said direct line, the Wabash from Post Vincents to the Ohio, by the Ohio, by a direct line, drawn due north from the mouth of the Great Miami, to the said territorial line, and by the said territorial line. The eastern State shall be bounded by the last mentioned direct line, the Ohio, Pennsylvania, and the said territorial line: Provided, however, and it is further understood and declared, that the boundaries of these three States shall be subject so far to be altered, that, if Congress shall hereafter find it expedient, they shall have authority to form one or two States in that part of the said territory which lies north of an east and west line drawn through the southerly bend or extreme of Lake Michigan. And, whenever any of the said States shall have sixty thousand free inhabitants therein, such State shall be admitted, by its delegates, into the Congress of the United States, on an equal footing with the original States in all respects whatever, and shall be at liberty to form a permanent constitution and State government: Provided, the constitution and government so to be formed, shall be republican, and in conformity to the principles contained in these articles; and, so far as it can be consistent with the general interest of the confederacy, such admission shall be allowed at an earlier period, and when there may be a less number of free inhabitants in the State than sixty thousand.

Article VI.

There shall be neither slavery nor involuntary servitude in the said territory, otherwise than in the punishment of crimes whereof the party shall have been duly convicted: Provided, always, That any person escaping into the same, from whom labor or service is lawfully claimed in any one of the original States, such fugitive may be lawfully reclaimed and conveyed to the person claiming his or her labor or service as aforesaid.

Be it ordained by the authority aforesaid, That the resolutions of the 23rd of April, 1784, relative to the subject of this ordinance, be, and the same are hereby repealed and declared null and void.

Done by the UNITED STATES in CONGRESS assembled, the 13th day of July, in the year of our Lord 1787, and of their sovereignty and independence the 12th.

The Bible in Schools

From a Letter of Dr. Benjamin Rush

Dr. Benjamin Rush (1745-1813) was one of the youngest signers of the Declaration of Independence in 1776. He was a distinguished physician and scientist who held the first chemistry professorship in America. He published the first American chemistry textbook, *A Syllabus of a Course of Lectures on Chemistry,* in 1770. He also established the first free dispensary in America in 1786 and published in 1812 the first American work on mental disorders, *Medical Inquiries and Observations Upon the Diseases of the Mind.* He also helped to found the first abolition society in America, The Society for the Relief of Free Negroes Unlawfully Held in Bondage, in 1775, and was appointed by President John Adams as the Treasurer of the United States Mint in 1797, which he held until 1813. The following is taken from a personal letter written by Dr. Rush in the late 1700s.

Dear Sir:

It is now several months since I promised to give you my reasons for preferring the Bible as a schoolbook to all other compositions. Before I state my arguments, I shall assume the five following propositions:

1. That Christianity is the only true and perfect religion; and that in proportion as mankind adopt its principals and obey its precepts they will be wise and happy.

2. That a better knowledge of this religion is to be acquired by reading the Bible than in any other way.

3. That the Bible contains more knowledge necessary to man in his present state than any other book in the world.

4. That knowledge is most durable, and religious instruction most useful, when imparted in early life.

5. That the Bible, when not read in schools, is seldom read in any subsequent period of life.

My arguments in favor of the use of the Bible as a schoolbook are founded,

I. In the constitution of the human mind.

1. The memory is the first faculty which opens in the minds of children. Of how much consequence, then, must it be to impress it with the great truths of Christianity, before it is preoccupied with less interesting subjects.

2. There is a peculiar aptitude in the minds of children for religious knowledge. I have constantly found them, in the first six or seven years of their lives, more inquisitive upon religious subjects than upon any others. And an ingenious instructor of youth has informed me that he has found young children more capable of receiving just ideas upon the most difficult tenets of religion than upon the most simple branches of human knowledge. It would be strange if it were otherwise, for God creates all His means to suit His ends. There must, of course, be a fitness between the human mind and the truths which are essential to its happiness.

3. The influence of early impressions is very great upon subsequent life; and in a world where false prejudices do so much mischief, it would discover great weakness not to oppose them by such as are true. I grant that many men have rejected the impressions derived from the Bible; but how much so ever these impressions may have been despised, I believe no man was ever early instructed in the truths of the Bible without having been

made wiser or better by the early operation of these impressions upon his mind. Every just principle that is to be found in the writings of Voltaire is borrowed from the Bible; and the morality of Deists, which has been so much admired and praised where it has existed, has been, I believe, in most cases, the effect of habits produced by early instruction in the principles of Christianity.

4. We are subject, by a general law of our natures, to what is called habit. Now, if the study of the Scriptures be necessary to our happiness at any time of our life, the sooner we begin to read them, the more we shall probably be attached to them; for it is peculiar to all the acts of habit, to become easy, strong, and agreeable by repetition.

5. It is a law on our natures that we remember longest the knowledge we acquire by the greatest number of our senses. Now, a knowledge of the contents of the Bible is acquired in school by the aid of the eye and the ear, for children, after getting their lessons, read or repeat them to their instructors in an audible voice; of course, there is a presumption that this knowledge will be retained much longer than if it had been acquired in any other way.

6. The interesting events and characters recorded and described in the Old and New Testaments are calculated, above all others, to seize upon all the faculties of the mind of children. The understanding, the memory, the imagination, the passions, and the moral powers are all occasionally addressed by the various incidents which are contained in those divine books, in so much that not to be delighted with them is to be devoid of every principle of pleasure that exists in a sound mind.

7. There is in man a native preference of truth to fiction. Lord Shaftesfury says that "truth is so congenial to our mind that we love even the shadow of it"; and Horace, in his rules for composing an epic poem, established the same law in our na-

tures by advising that "fictions on poetry should resemble truth." Now, the Bible contains more truth than any other book in the world; so true is the testimony that it bears of God in His works of creation, providence, and redemption that it is called truth itself, by way of preeminence above other things that are acknowledged to be true. How forcibly are we struck with the evidence of truth in the history of the Jews, above what we discover in the history of other nations. Where do we find a hero of an historian record his own faults or vices except in the Old Testament? Indeed, my friend, from some accounts which I have read of the American Revolution, I begin to grown skeptical to all history except that which is contained in the Bible. Now, if this book be known to contain nothing but what is materially true, the mind will naturally acquire a love for it from this affection for the truths of the Bible, it will acquire a discernment of truth in other books, and a preference of it in all the transactions of life.

8. There is wonderful property in the memory which enables it in old age to recover the knowledge acquired in early life after it had been apparently forgotten for forty or fifty years. Of how much consequence, then, must it be to fill the mind with that species of knowledge in childhood and youth which, when recalled in the decline of life, will support the soul under the infirmities of age and smooth the avenues of approaching death. The Bible is the only book which is capable of affording this support to old age; and it is for this reason that we find it resorted to with so much diligence and pleasure by such old people as have read it in early life. I can recollect many instances of this kind in persons who discovered no special attachment to the Bible in the meridian of their days, who have, notwithstanding, spent the evening of life in reading no other book. The late Sir John Pringle, physician to the queen of Great Britain, after passing a long life in camps and at court, closed it by studying the

Scriptures. So anxious was he to increase his knowledge in them that he wrote to Dr. Michaelis, a learned professor of divinity in Germany, for an explanation of a difficult text of Scripture a short time before his death.

II. My second argument in favor of the use of the Bible in schools is founded upon an implied command of God and upon the practice of several of the wisest nations of the world.

In the sixth chapter of Deuteronomy, we find the following words, which are directly to my purpose: "And thou shalt love the LORD thy God with all thine heart, and with all thy soul, and with all thy might. And these words, which I command thee this day, shall be in thine heart: And thou shalt teach them diligently unto thy children, and shalt talk of them when thou sittest in thine house, and when thou walkest by the way, and when thou liest down, and when thou risest up."

It appears, moreover, from the history of the Jews, that they flourished as a nation in proportion as they honored and read the books of Moses, which contained the only revelation that God had made to the world. The law was not only neglected, but lost, during the general profligacy of manner which accompanied the long and wicked reign of Manasseh. But the discovery of it amid the rubbish of the temple by Josiah and its subsequent general use were followed by a return of national virtue and prosperity. We read further of the wonderful effects which the reading of the law by Ezra, after his return from his captivity in Babylon, had upon the Jews. They hung upon his lips with tears, and showed the sincerity of their repentance by their general reformation.

The learning of the Jews, for many years, consisted in a knowledge of the Scriptures. These were the textbooks of all the instruction that was given in the schools of their Prophets. It was by means of this general knowledge of their law that those Jews who wandered from Judea into other countries carried with them and propagated certain ideas of the true God among all the civilized nations upon the face of the earth. And it was from the attachment they retained to the Old Testament that they procured a translation of it into the Greek language, after they had lost the Hebrew tongue by their long absence from their native country. The utility of this translation, commonly called the Septuagint, in facilitating the progress of the Gospel is well known to all who are acquainted with the history of the first age of the Christian church.

But the benefits of an early and general acquaintance with the Bible were not confined to the Jewish nation; they have appeared in many countries in Europe since the Reformation. The industry and habits of order which distinguish many of the German nations are derived from their early instruction in the principles of Christianity by means of the Bible. In Scotland and in parts of New England, where the Bible has been long used as a schoolbook, the inhabitants are among the most enlightened in religions and science, the most strict in morals, and the most intelligent in human affairs of any people whose history has come to my knowledge upon the surface of the globe.

I wish to be excused from repeating here that if the Bible did not convey a single direction for the attainment of future happiness, it should be read in our schools in preference to all other books from its containing the greatest portion of that kind of knowledge which is calculated to produce private and public temporal happiness.

We err, not only in human affairs but in religion likewise, only because we do not "know the Scriptures" and obey their instructions. Immense truths, I believe, are concealed in them. The time, I have no doubt, will come when posterity will view and pity our ignorance of these truths as much as we do the ignorance sometimes manifested by the disciples of our Saviour, who knew nothing of the meaning of those plain passages in the Old Testament which were daily fulfilling before their eyes.

But further, we err, not only in religion but in philosophy likewise, because we "do not know or believe the Scriptures." The sciences have been compared to a circle, of which religion composes a part. To understand any one of them perfectly, it is necessary to have some knowledge of them all. Bacon, Boyle, and Newton included the Scriptures in the inquiries to which their universal geniuses disposed them, and their philosophy was aided by their knowledge in them. A striking agreement has been lately discovered between the history of certain events recorded in the Bible and some of the operations and productions of nature, particularly those which are related in Whitehurst's observation on the deluge, in Smith's account of the origin of the variety of color in the human species, and in Bruce's travels. It remains yet to be shown how many other events related in the Bible accord with some late important discoveries in the principles alluded to mutually establish the truth of each other.

I know it is said that the familiar use of the Bible in our schools has a tendency to lessen a due reverence for it. But this objection, by proving too much, proves nothing. If familiarity lessens respect for divine things, then all those precepts of our religion which enjoin the daily or weekly worship of the Deity are improper. The Bible was not intended to represent a Jewish ark; and it is an anti-Christian idea to suppose that it can be profaned by being carried into a schoolhouse, or by being handled by children.

It is also said that a great part of the Old Testament is no way interesting to mankind under the present dispensation of the Gospel. But I deny that any of the books of the Old Testament are not interesting to mankind under the Gospel dispensation. Most of the characters, events, and ceremonies mentioned in them are personal, providential, or instituted types of the Messiah, all of which have been, or remain yet, to be fulfilled by Him. It is from an ignorance or neglect of these types that we have so many Deists in Christendom, for so irrefragably do they prove the truth of Christianity that I am sure a young man who had been regularly instructed in their meaning could never doubt afterwards of the truth of any of its principles. If any obscurity appears in these principles, it is only, to use the words of the poet, because they are dark with excessive brightness.

I know there is an objection among many people to teaching children doctrines of any kind, because they are liable to be converted. But let us not be wiser than our Maker. If moral precepts alone could have reformed mankind, the mission of the Son of God into our world would have been unnecessary. He came to promulgate a system of doctrines, as well as a system of morals. The perfect morality of the Gospel rests upon a doctrine which, though often controverted, has never been refuted; I mean the vicarious life and death of the Son of God. This sublime and ineffable doctrine delivers us from the absurd hypothesis of modern philosophers concerning the foundation of moral obligation, and fixes it upon the eternal and self-moving principle of Love. It concentrates a whole system of ethics in a single text of Scripture: "A new commandment I give unto you, that ye love one another, even as I have loved you." By withholding the knowledge of this doctrine from children, we deprive ourselves of the best means of awakening moral sensibility in their minds. We do more; we furnish an argument for withholding from them a knowledge of the morality of the Gospel likewise; for this, in many instances, is as supernatural, and therefore as liable to be controverted, as any of the doctrines or miracles which are mentioned in the New Testament. The miraculous conception of the Saviour of the world by a virgin is not more opposed to the ordinary course of natural events, nor is the doctrine of the atonement more above human reason, than those moral precepts which command us to love our enemies or to die for our friends.

I cannot but suspect that the present fashionable practice of rejecting the Bible from our schools has originated with Deists. And they discover great ingenuity in this mode of attacking Christianity. If they proceed in it, they will do more in half a century in extirpating our religion than Bolingbroke or Voltaire could have effected in a thousand years.

But passing by all other considerations, and contemplating merely the political institutions of the United States, I lament that we waste so much time and money in punishing crimes and take so little pains to prevent them. We profess to be republicans, and yet we neglect the only means of establishing and perpetuating our republican forms of government; that is, the universal education of our youth in the principles of Christianity by means of the Bible; for this divine book, above all others, favors that equality among mankind, that respect for just laws, and all those sober and frugal virtues which constitute the soul of republicanism.

Perhaps an apology may be necessary for my having presumed to write upon a subject so much above my ordinary studies. My excuse for it is that I thought a single mite from a member for a profession which has been frequently charged with skepticism in religion might attract the notice of persons who had often overlooked the more ample contributions, upon this subject, of gentlemen in other professions.

With great respect, I am, etc.
Benjamin Bush

Used by permission of the American Tract Society. For free samples or catalog, call 1-800-54-TRACT.

Letter to Hillary Clinton

11 November 1992

Hillary Clinton
The Governor's Mansion
1800 Canter Street
Little Rock, AR 72206

Dear Hillary:

I still cannot believe you won. But utter delight that you did pervades all the circles in which I move. I met last Wednesday in David Rockefeller's office with him, John Sculley, Dave Barram, and David Heselkorn. It was a great celebration. Both John and David R. were more expansive than I have ever seen them—literally radiating happiness. My own view and theirs is that this country has seized its last chance. I am fond of quoting Winston Churchill to the effect that "America always does the right thing—after it has exhausted all the alternatives." This election, more than anything else in my experience, proves his point.

The subject we were discussing was what you and Bill should do now about education, training, and labor market policy. Following that meeting, I chaired another in Washington on the same topic. Those present at the second meeting included Tim Barnicle, Dave Barram, Mike Cohen, David Hornbeck, Hillary Pennington, Andy Plattner, Lauren Resnick, Betsy Brown Ruzzi, Bob Schwartz, Mike Smith, and Bill Spring. Shirley Malcolm,

Ray Marshall, and Susan McGuire were also invited. Though these three were not able to be present at last week's meeting, they have all contributed by telephone to the ideas that follow. Ira Magaziner was also invited to this meeting.

Our purpose in these meetings was to propose concrete actions that the Clinton administration could take—between now and the inauguration, in the first one hundred days and beyond. The result, from where I sit, was really exciting. We took a very large leap forward in terms of how to advance the agenda on which you and we have all been working—a practical plan for putting all the major components of the system in place within four years, by the time Bill has to run again.

I take personal responsibility for what follows. Though I believe everyone involved in the planning effort is in broad agreement, they may not all agree on the details. You should also be aware that, although the plan comes from a group closely associated with the National Center of Education and the Economy, there was no practical way to poll our whole Board on this plan in the time available. It represents, then, not a proposal from our Center, but the best thinking of the group I have named.

We think the great opportunity you have is to remold the entire American System for human resources development, almost all of the current components of which were put in place before World War II. The danger is that Bill advanced in the campaign in the area of education and training could be translated individually in the ordinary course of governing into a legislative proposal and enacted as a program. This is the plan of least resistance. But it will lead to these programs being grafted onto the present system, not to a new system, and the opportunity will have been lost. If this sense of time and place is correct, it is essential that the administration's efforts be guided by a consistent vision of what it were to accomplish in the field of human resource development, with respect both of choice of key officials and the program.

What follows comes in three places:

First, a vision of the kind of national—not federal—human resources development system the nation could have. This is interwoven with a new approach to governing that should inform that vision. What is essential is that we create a seamless web of opportunities, to develop one's skills that literally extends from cradle to grave and is the same system for everyone—young and old, poor and rich, worker and full-time student. It needs to be a system driven by client's needs (not agency regulations or the needs of the organization providing services), guided by clear standards that define the stages of the system for the people who progress through it, and regulated on the basis of outcomes that providers produce for their clients, not inputs into the system.

Second, a proposed legislative agenda you can use to implement this vision. We propose four high priority packages that will enable you to move quickly on the campaign promises:

1. The first would use your proposal for an apprenticeship system as the keystone of a strategy for putting a whole new postsecondary training system in place. That system would incorporate your proposal for reforming postsecondary education finance. It contains what we think is a powerful idea for rolling out and scaling up the whole new human resources system nationwide over the next four years, using the (renamed) apprenticeship ideas as the entering wedge.

2. The second would combine initiatives on dislocated workers, a rebuilt employment service and a new system of labor market boards to offer the Clinton administration's employment security program, built on the best practices anywhere in the world. This is the backbone of a system for

assuring adult workers in our society that they need never again watch with dismay as their jobs disappear and their chances of ever getting a good job again go with them.

3. The third would concentrate on the overwhelming problems of our inner cities, combining elements of the first and second packages into a special program to greatly raise the work-related skills of the people trapped in the core of our great cities.

4. The fourth would enable you to take advantage of legislation on which Congress has already been working to advance the elementary and secondary reform agenda.

The other major proposal we offer has to do with government organization for the human resources agenda. While we share your reservations about the hazards involved in bringing reorganization proposals to the Congress, we believe that the one we have come up with minimizes those drawbacks while creating an opportunity for the new administration to move like lightning to implement its human resources development proposals. We hope you can consider the merits of this idea quickly, because, if you decide to go with it or something like it, it will greatly affect the nature of the offers you make to prospective cabinet members.

The Vision

We take the proposals Bill put before the country in the campaign to be utterly consistent with the ideas advanced in America's Choice, the school restructuring agenda first stated in *A Nation Prepared,* and later incorporated in the work of the National Alliance for Restructuring Education, and the elaboration of this view that Ray and I tried to capture in our book, *Thinking for a Living.* Taken together, we think these ideas constitute a consistent vision for a new human resources development system for the United States. I have tried to capture the essence of that vision below.

An Economic Strategy Based on Skill Development

- The economy's strength is derived from a whole population as skilled as any in the world, working in workplaces organized to take maximum advantage of the skills those people have to offer.
- A seamless system of unending skill development that begins in the home with the very young and continues through school, postsecondary education and the workplace.

The Schools

- Clear national standards of performance in general education (the knowledge and skills that everyone is expected to hold in common) are set to the level of the best achieving nations in the world for students of sixteen, and public schools are expected to bring all but the most severely handicapped up to that standard. Students get a certificate when they meet this standard, allowing them to go on to the next stage of their education. Though the standards are set to international benchmarks, they are distinctly American, reflecting our needs and values.
- We have a national system of education in which curriculum, pedagogy, examinations, and teacher education and licensure-systems are all linked to the national standards, but which provides for substantial variance among states, districts, and schools on these matters. This new system of linked standards, curriculum, and pedagogy will abandon the American tracking system, combining high academic standards with the ability to apply what one knows to real world problems, and qualifying all students to a lifetime of learning in the postsecondary system and at work.
- We have a system that rewards students who meet the national standards with further education and good jobs, providing

them a strong incentive to work hard in school.

- Our public school systems are reorganized to free up school professionals to make the key decisions about how to use all the available resources to bring students up to the standards. Most of the federal, state, district, and union rules and regulations that now restrict school professional ability to make these decisions are swept away, though strong measures are in place to make sure that vulnerable populations get the help they need. School professionals are paid at a level comparable to that of other professionals, but they are expected to put in a full year, to spend whatever time it takes to do the job, and to be fully accountable for the results of their work. The federal, state, and local governments provide the time, staff development resources, technology, and other support needed for them to do the job. Nothing less than a wholly restructured school system can possibly bring all of our students up to the standards only a few have been expected to meet up to now.

- There is a real—aggressive—program of public choice in our schools, rather than the flaccid version that is widespread now.

- All students are guaranteed that they will have a fair shot at reaching the standards: that is, that whether they make it or not depends on the effort they are willing to make, and nothing else. "School delivery standards" are in place to make sure this happens. These standards have the same status in the system as the new student performance standards, assuring that the quality of instruction is high everywhere, but they are fashioned so as not to constitute a new bureaucratic nightmare.

Postsecondary Education and Work Skills

- All students who meet the new national standards for general education are entitled to the equivalent of three more years of free additional education. We would have the federal and state governments match funds to guarantee one free year of college education to everyone who meets the new national standards for general education. So a student who meets the standard at sixteen would be entitled to two free years of high school and one of college. Loans, which can be forgiven for public service, are available for additional education beyond that. National standards for sub-baccalaureate college-level professional and technical degrees and certificates will be established with the participation of employers, labor, and higher education. These programs will include both academic study and structured on-the-job training. Eighty percent or more of American high school graduates will be expected to get some form of college degree, though most of them less than a baccalaureate. These new professional and technical certificates and degrees typically are won within three years of acquiring the general education certificate, so, for most postsecondary students, college will be free. These professional and technical degree programs will be designed to link to programs leading to the baccalaureate degree and higher degrees. There will be no dead ends in this system. Everyone who meets the general education standard will be able to go to some form of college, being able to borrow all the money they need to do so, beyond the first free year.

This idea of post-secondary professionals and technical certificates captures all of the essentials of the apprenticeship idea, while offering none of its drawbacks (see below). But it also makes clear that those engaged in apprentice-style programs are getting more than narrow training; they are continuing their education for other purposes as well, and building a base for more education later. Clearly, this idea redefines college. Proprietary schools, employers and community-based organizations will want to offer these programs, as well as community colleges and four-year institutions, but these new entrants will have to be accredited if they are to qualify to offer the programs.

- Employers are not required to provide slots for the structured on-the-job training component of the program but many do so, because they get first access to the most accomplished graduates of these programs, and they can use these programs to introduce the trainees to their own values and way of doing things.

- The system of skill standards for technical and professional degrees is the same for students just coming out of high school and for adults in the workforce. It is progressive, in the sense that certificates and degrees for entry level jobs lead to further professional and technical education programs at higher levels. Just as in the case of the system for the schools, though the standards are the same everywhere (leading to maximum mobility for students), the curricula can vary widely and programs can be custom designed to fit the needs of full-time and part-time students with very different requirements. Government grant and loan programs are available on the same terms to full-time and part-time students, as long as the programs in which they are enrolled are designed to lead to certificates and degrees defined by the system of professional and technical standards.

- The national system of professional and technical standards is designed much like the multistate bar, which provides a national core around which of the states can specify additional standards that meet their unique needs. There are national standards and exams for no more than twenty broad occupational areas, each of which can lead to many occupations in a number of related industries. Students who qualify in any one of these areas have the broad skills required by a whole family of occupations, and most are sufficiently skilled to enter the workforce immediately with further occupation-specific skills provided by their union or employer. Industry and occupational groups can voluntarily create standards building in these broad standards for their own needs, as can the states. Students entering the system are first introduced to very broad occupational groups, narrowing over time to concentrate on acquiring the skills needed for a cluster of occupations. This modular system provides for the initiative of particular states and occupations by reducing the time and cost entailed in moving from one occupation to another. In this way, a balance is established between the kinds of generic skills needed to function effectively in high performance work organizations and the skills needed to continue learning quickly and well through a lifetime of work, on the one hand, and the specific skills needed to perform at a high level in a particular occupation on the other.

Institutions receiving grant and loan funds under this system are required to provide information to the public and to government agencies in a uniform format. This information covers enrollment by program, costs, and success rates for students of different backgrounds, and characteristics, and career outcomes for those students, thereby enabling students to make informed choices among institutions based on cost and performance. Loan defaults are reduced to a level close to zero, both because programs that do not deliver what they promise are not selected by prospective students and because the new postsecondary loan system uses the IRS to collect what is owed from salaries and wages as they are earned.

Education and Training for Employed and Unemployed Adults

- The national system of skills standards establishes the basis for the development of a coherent, unified training system.

That system can be accessed by students coming out of high school, employed adults who want to improve their prospects, unemployment adults who are dislocated and others who lack the basic skills required to get out of poverty. But it is all the same system. There are no longer any parts of it that are exclusively for the disadvantaged, though special measures are taken to make sure that the disadvantaged are served. It is a system for everyone, just as all the parts of the system already described are for everyone. So the people who take advantage of this system are not marked by it as "damaged goods." The skills they acquire are world class, clear, and defined in part by the employers who will make decisions about hiring and advancement.

The new general education standard becomes the target for all basic educational programs, both for school dropouts and adults. Achieving that standard is the prerequisite for enrollment in all professional and technical degree programs. A wide range of agencies and institutions offer programs leading to the general education certificate, including high schools, dropout recovery centers, adult education centers, community colleges, prisons, and employers. These programs are tailored to the needs of the people who enroll in them. All the programs receiving government grant or loan funds that come with dropouts and adults for enrollment in programs preparing students to meet the general education standard must release the same kind of data required of the postsecondary institutions on enrollment, program description, cost, and success rates. Reports are produced for each institution and for the system as a whole showing differential success rates for each major demographic group.

- The system is funded in four different ways, all providing access to the same or a similar set of services. School dropouts below the age of twenty-one are entitled to the same amount of funding from the same sources that they would have been entitled to had they stayed in school. Dislocated workers are funded through the federal government through the federal programs for that purpose and by state unemployment insurance funds. The chronically unemployed are funded by the federal and state funds established for that purpose. Employed people can access the system through the requirement that their employers spend an amount equal to one and one-half percent of their salary and wage bill on training leading to national skill certification. People in prison could get reductions in their sentences by meeting the general education standard in a program provided by the prison system. Any of these groups can also use the funds in their individual training account, if they have any, the balances in their grant entitlement, or their access to the student loan fund.

Labor Market Systems

- The Employment Service is greatly upgraded and separated from the Unemployment Insurance Fund. All available front-line jobs—whether public or private—must be listed in it by law. This provision must be carefully designed to make sure that employers will not be subject to employment suits based on the data produced by this system—if they are subject to such suits, they will not participate. All trainees in the system looking for work are entitled to be listed in it without a fee. So it is no longer a system just for the poor and unskilled, but for everyone. The system is fully computerized. It lists not only job openings and job seekers (with their qualifications) but also all the institutions in the labor market area offering programs leading to the general education certificate and those offering programs leading to the professional and technical college degrees and certificates, along with all the relevant data about the costs, characteristics, and performance of those programs—for everyone and for special populations. Counselors are available to any citizen to help them assess their needs, plan a program, and finance it, and once they are trained, to find an opening.

- A system of labor market boards is established at the local, state, and federal levels to coordinate the systems for job training, postsecondary professional and technical education, adult basic education, job matching, and counseling. The rebuilt Employment Service is supervised by these boards. The system's clients no longer have to go from agency to agency filling out separate applications for separate programs. It is all taken care of at the local labor market board office by one counselor accessing the integrated computer-based program, which makes it possible for the counselor to determine eligibility for all relevant programs at once, plan a program with the client, and assemble the necessary funding from all the available sources. The same system will enable counselor and client to array all the relevant program providers side by side, access their relative costs and performance records, and determine which providers are best to meet the client's needs based on performance.

Some Common Features

- Throughout, the object is to have a performance-and-client-oriented system to encourage local creativity and responsibility by getting local people to commit to high goals and organize to achieve them, sweeping away as much of the rules, regulations, and bureaucracy that are in their way as possible, provided that they are making real progress against their goals. For this to work, the standards at every level of the system have to be clear: every client has to know what they have to accomplish in order to get what they want out of the system. The service providers have to be supported in the task of getting their clients to the finish line and rewarded when they are making real progress toward that goal. We would sweep away means-tested programs, because they stigmatize their recipients and alienate the public, replacing them with programs that are for everyone, but also work for the disadvantage. We would replace rules defining inputs with rules defining outcomes and rewards for achieving them. This means, among other things, permitting local people to combine as many federal programs as they see fit, provided that the intended beneficiaries are progressing toward the right outcomes (there are now twenty-three separate federal programs for dislocated workers). We would make individuals, their families, and whole communities the unit of service, not agencies, programs, and projects. Wherever possible, we would have service providers compete with one another for funds that come with the client, in an environment in which the client has good information about the cost and performance record of the competing providers. Dealing with public agencies—whether they are schools or the employment service—should be more like dealing with Federal Express than with the old Post Office.

This vision, as I pointed out above, is consistent with everything Bill proposed as a candidate. But it goes beyond those proposals, extending them from ideas for new programs to a comprehensive vision of how they can be used as building blocks, or a whole new system. But this vision is very complex, will take a long time to sell, and will have to be revised many times along the way. The right way to think about it is as an internal working document that forms the background for a plan, not the plan itself. One would want to make sure that the specific actions of the new administration were designed, in a general way, to advance this agenda as it evolved while not committing anyone to the details, which would change over time.

Everything that follows is cast in the frame of strategies for bringing the new system into being, not as a pilot program, not as a few demonstrations to be swept aside in another administration, but everywhere, as the new way of doing business.

In the sections that follow, we break these goals down into their main components and propose an action plan for each.

Major Components of the Program

The preceding section presented a vision of the system we have in mind chronologically from the point of view of an individual served by it. Here we reverse the order, starting with descriptions of program components designed to serve adults, and working our way down to the very young.

High Skills for Economic Competitiveness Program

Developing System Standards

- Create National Board for Professional and Technical Standards. Board is private not-for-profit chartered by Congress. Charter specifies broad membership composed of leading figures from higher education, business, labor, government, and advocacy groups. Board can receive appropriated funds from Congress, private foundations, individuals, and corporations. Neither Congress nor the executive branch can dictate the standards set by the Board. But the Board is required to report annually to the President and the Congress in order to provide for public accountability. It is also directed to work collaboratively with the states and cities involved in the Collaborative Design and Development Program (see below) in the development of the standards.

  Charter specifies that the National Board will set broad performance standards (not time-in-the-seat standards or course standards) for college-level Professional and Technical certificates and degrees in not more than twenty areas and develops performance examinations for each. The Board is required to set broad standards of the kind described in the vision statement above and is not permitted to simply refly the narrow standards that characterize many occupations now. (More than two thousand standards currently exist, many for licensed occupations—these are not the kinds of standards we have in mind.) It also specifies that the programs leading to these certificates and degrees will combine time in the classroom with time at the work-site in structured on-the-job training. The standards assume the existence of (high school level) general education standards set by others. The new standards and exams are meant to be supplemented by the states and by individual industries and occupations. Board is responsible for administering the exam system and continually updating the standards and exams.

Legislation creating the Board is sent to the Congress in the first six months of the administration, imposing a deadline for creating the standards and the exams within three years of passage of the legislation.

Commentary

The proposal reframes the Clinton apprenticeship proposal as a college program and establishes a mechanism for setting the standards for the program. The unions are adamantly opposed to broad based apprenticeship programs by that name. Focus groups conducted by JFF and others show that parents everywhere want their kids to go to college, not to be shunted aside into a non-college apprenticeship "vocational" program. By requiring these programs to be a combination of classroom instruction and structured OUT; and creating a standard-setting board that includes employers and labor, all the objectives of the apprenticeship idea are achieved, while at the same time assuring much broader support for the idea, as well as a guarantee that the program will not become too narrowly focused on particular occupations. It also ties the Clinton apprenticeship idea to the Clinton college funding proposal in a seamless web. Charging the Board with creating not more than twenty certificate or degree categories establishes a balance between the need to create one national system on the one hand with the need to avoid creating a cumbersome and rigid national bureaucracy on the other. This approach provides lots of latitude for individual industry groups, professional groups and state authorities to establish their own standards, while at the same time avoiding the chaos that would surely occur if they were the only source of standards. The bill establishing the Board should also authorize the executive branch to make grants to industry groups, professional societies, occupational groups, and states to develop standards and exams. Our assumption is that the system we are proposing will be managed so as to encourage the states to combine the last two years of high school and the first two years of community college into three year programs leading to college degrees and certificates. Proprietary institutions, employers, and community-based organizations could also offer these programs, but they would have to be accredited to offer these college-level programs. Eventually, students getting their general education certificates might go directly to community college or to another form of college, but the new system should not require that.

Collaborative Design and Development Program

The object is to create a single comprehensive system for professional and technical education that meets the requirements of everyone from high school students to skilled dislocated workers, from the hard core unemployed to employed adults who want to improve their prospects. Creating such a system means sweeping aside countless programs, building new ones, combining funding authorities, changing deeply embedded institutional structures, and so on. The question is how to get from where we are to where we want to be. Trying to ram it down everyone's throat would engender overwhelming opposition. Our idea is to draft legislation that would offer an opportunity for those states—and selected large cities—that are excited about this set of ideas to come forward and join with each other and with the federal government in an alliance to do the necessary design work and actually deliver the needed services on a fast track. The legislation would require the executive branch to establish a competitive grant program for these states and cities and to engage a group of organizations to offer technical assistance to the expanding set of states and cities engaged in designing and implementing the new system. This is not the usual large scale experiment, nor is it a demonstration program. A highly regarded precedent exists for this approach in the National Science Foundation's SSI program. As soon as the first set of states is engaged, another set would be invited to participate, until most or all states are involved. It is a collaborative design, rollout and scale-up program. It is intended to parallel the work of the National Board for College Professional and Technical Standards, so that the states and cities (and all their partners) would be able to implement the new standards as soon they become available, although they would be delivering services on a large scale before that happened. Thus, major parts of the whole system would be in operation in a majority of the states within three years from the passage of the initial legislation. Inclusion of selected large cities in this design is not an afterthought. We believe that what we are proposing here for the cities is the necessary complement to a large scale job-creation program for the cities. Skill development will not work if there are no jobs, but job development will not work without a determined effort to improve the skills of city residents. This is the skill development component.

- Participants
  - Volunteer states, counterpart initiative for cities
  - Fifteen states, fifteen cities selected to begin in first year. fifteen more in each successive year.
  - Five year grants (on the order of $20 million per year to each state, lower amounts of the cities) given to each, with specific goals to be achieved by the third year, including program elements in place (e.g., upgraded employment service), number of people enrolled in new professional and technical programs and so on.
  - A core set of High Performance Work Organization firms willing to participate in standard setting and to offer training slots and mentors.

- Criteria for Selection
  - Strategies for enriching existing co-op tech prep and other programs to meet the criteria.
  - Commitment to implementing new general education standard in legislation.
  - Commitment to implementing the new Technical and Professional skills standards for college.
  - Commitment to developing an outcome and performance-based system for human resources development system.
  - Commitment to new role for employment service.
  - Commitment to join with others in national design and implementation activity.

- Clients
  - young adults entering workforce
  - dislocated workers

- long-term unemployed
- employed who want to upgrade skills

- Program Components
  - Institute own version of state and local labor market boards. Local labor market boards to involve leading employers, labor representatives, educators, and advocacy group leaders in running the redesigned employment service, running intake system for all clients, counseling all clients, maintaining the information system that will make the vendor market efficient, and organizing employers to provide job experience and training slots for school youth and adult trainees.
  - Rebuild employment service as a primary function of labor market boards.
  - Develop programs to bring dropouts and illiterates up to general education certificate standard. Organize local alternative providers, firms to provide alternative education, counseling, job experience, and placement services to these clients.
  - Development programs for dislocated workers and hard-core unemployed (see below).
  - Develop city and state-wide programs to combine the last two years of high school and the first two years of colleges into three-year programs after acquisition of the general education certificate to culminate in college certificates and degrees. These programs should combine academic and structure on-the-job training.
  - Develop uniform reporting system for providers, requiring them to provide information in that format on characteristics of clients, their success rates by program, and the costs of those programs. Develop computer-based system for combining this data at local labor market board offices with

employment data from the state so that counselors and clients can look at programs offered by colleges and other vendors in terms of cost, client characteristics, program design, and outcomes. Including subsequent employment histories for graduates.

- Design all programs around the forthcoming general education standards and the standards to be developed by the National Board for College Professional and Technical Standards.

- Create statewide program of technical assistance to firms on high performance work organization and help them develop quality programs for participants in Technical and Professional certificate and degree programs. (It is essential that these programs be high quality, nonbureaucratic, and voluntary for the firms.)

- Participate with other states and the national technical assistance program in the national alliance effort to exchange information and assistance among all participants.

- National technical assistance to participants
  - Executive branch authorized to compete opportunity to provide the following services (probably using a Request for Qualifications):
    - State-of-the art assistance to the states and cities related to the principal program components (e.g., work reorganization, training, basic literacy, funding systems, apprenticeship systems, large scale data management systems, training systems for the HR professional who make the whole system work, etc.). A number of organizations would be funded. Each would be expected to provide information and direct assistance to the states and cities involved, and to coordinate their efforts with one another.

- It is essential that the technical assistance function include a major professional development component to make sure the key people in the states and cities upon whom success depends have the resources available to develop the high skills required. Some of the funds for this function should be provided directly to the states and cities, some to the technical assistance agency.
- Coordination of the design and implementation activities of the whole consortium, document results, prepare reports, etc. One organization would be funded to perform this function.

Dislocated Workers Program

- New legislation would permit combining all dislocated workers programs at redesigned employment service office. Clients would, in effect, receive vouchers for education and training in amounts determined by the benefits for which they qualify. Employment service case managers would qualify client worker for benefits and assist the client in the selection of education and training programs offered by provider institutions. Any provider institutions that receive funds derived from dislocated worker programs are required to provide information on costs and performance of programs in uniform format described above. This consolidated and voucherized dislocated workers program would operate nationwide. It would be integrated with Collaborative Design and Development Program in those states and cities in which that program functioned. It would be built around the general education certificate and the Professional and Technical Certificate and Degree Program as soon as those standards were in place. In this way, programs for dislocated workers would be progressively and fully integrated with the rest of the national education and training system.

Levy Grant System

- This is the part of the system that provides funds for currently employed people to improve their skills. Ideally, it should specifically provide means whereby frontline workers can earn their general education credential (if they do not already have one) and acquire Professional and Technical Certificates and Degrees in fields of their choosing.

- Everything we have heard indicates virtually universal opposition in the employer community to the proposal for a one and one-half percent levy on employers for training to support the costs associated with employed workers gaining these skills, whatever the levy is called. We propose that Bill take a leaf out of the German book. One of the most important reasons that large German employers offer apprenticeship slots to German youngsters is that they fear, with good reason, that if they don't volunteer to do so, the law will require it. Bill could gather a group of leading executives and business organization leaders, and tell them straight out that he will hold back on submitting legislation to require a training levy, provided that they commit themselves to a drive to get employers to get their average expenditures on frontline employee training up to two percent of frontline employee salaries and wages within two years. If they have not done so within that time, then he will expect their support when he submits legislation requiring the training levy. He could do the same thing with respect to slots for structured on-the-job training.

College Loan/Public Service Program

- We presume that this program is being designed by others and so have not attended to it. From everything we know about it, however, it is entirely compatible with the rest of what is proposed here. What is, of course, especially relevant here, is that our reconceptualization of the apprenticeship proposal as a college-level education program, combined with our proposal that everyone who gets the general education credential be entitled to a free year of higher education (combined federal and state funds) will have a decided impact on the calculations of cost for the college loan/ public service program.

Assistance for Dropouts and the Long Term Unemployed

- The problem of upgrading the skills of high school dropouts and the adult hard core unemployed is especially difficult. It is also at the heart of the problem of our inner cities. All the evidence indicates that what is needed is something with all the important characteristics of a nonresidential Job Corps-like program. The problem with the Job Corps is that it is operated directly by the federal government and is therefore not embedded at all in the infrastructure of local communities. The way to solve this program is to create a new urban program that is locally—not federally—organized and administered, but which must operate in a way that uses something like the federal standards for contracting for Job Corps services. In this way, local employers, neighborhood organizations, and other local service providers could meet the need, but requiring local authorities to use the federal standards would assure high quality results. Programs for high school dropouts and the hard-core unemployed would probably have to be separately organized, though the services provided would be much the same. Federal funds would be offered on a matching basis with state and local funds for this purpose. These programs should be fully integrated with the revitalized employment service. The local labor market board would be the local authority responsible for receiving the funds and contracting with providers for the services. It would provide diagnostic, placement, and testing services. We would eliminate the targeted jobs credit and use the money now spent on that program to finance these operations. Funds can also be used from the JOBS program in the welfare reform act. This will not be sufficient, however, because there is currently no federal money available to meet the needs of hard-core unemployment males (mostly black) and so new monies will have to be appropriated for the purpose.

Commentary

As you know very well, the High Skills: Competitive Workforce as sponsored by Senators Kennedy and Hatfield and Congressman Gephardt and Regula provides a ready-made vehicle for advancing many of the ideas we have outlined. To foster a good working relationship with the Congress, we suggest that, to the extent possible, the framework of these companion bills be used to frame the President's proposals. You may not know that we have put together a large group of representatives of Washington-based organizations to come to a consensus around the ideas in America's Choice. They are full of energy and very committed to this joint effort. If they are made part of the process of framing the legislative proposals, they can be expected to be strong support for them when they arrive on the Hill. As you think about the assembly of these ideas into specific legislative proposals, you may also want to take into account the packaging ideas that come later in this letter.

Elementary and Secondary Education Program

The situation with respect to elementary and secondary education is very different from adult education and training. In the latter case, a new vision and a whole new structure is required. In the former, there is increasing acceptance of a new vision and structure among the public at large, within the relevant professional groups and in Congress. There is also a lot of existing activity on which to build. So we confine ourselves here to describing some of those activities that can be used to launch the Clinton education program.

Standard Setting

Legislation to accelerate the process of national standard setting in education was contained in the conference report on S.2 and HR 4323 that was defeated on a recent cloture vote. Solid majorities were behind the legislation in both houses of Congress. While some of us would quarrel with a few of the details, we think the new administration should support the early reintroduction of this legislation with whatever changes it thinks fit. This legislation does not establish a national body to create a national examination system. We think that is the right choice for now.

Systemic Change in Public Education

The conference report on S.2 and HR 4323 also contained a comprehensive program to support systemic change in public education. Here again, some of us would quibble with some of the particulars, but we believe that the administration's objectives would be well served by endorsing the resubmission of this legislation, modified as it sees fit.

Federal Programs for the Disadvantaged

The established federal education programs for the disadvantaged need to be thoroughly overhauled to reflect an emphasis on results for the student rather than compliance with the regulations. A national commission on Chapter 1, the largest of these programs, chaired by David Hornbeck, has designed a radically new version of the legislation, with the active participation of many of the advocacy groups. Other groups have been similarly engaged. We think the new administration should quickly endorse the work of the national commission and introduce its proposals early next year. It is unlikely that this legislation will pass before the deadline—two years away—for the reauthorization of the Elementary and Secondary Education Act, but early endorsement of this new approach by the administration will send a strong signal to the Congress and will greatly affect the climate in which other parts of the act will be considered.

Public Choice Technology, Integrated Health and Human Services, Curriculum Resources, High Performance Management, Professional Development, and Research and Development

The restructuring of the schools that is envisioned in S.2 and HR 4323 is not likely to succeed unless the schools have a lot of information about how to do it and real assistance in getting it done. The areas in which this help is needed are suggested by the heading of this section. One of the most cost-effective things the federal government could do is to provide support for research, development, and technical assistance of the schools on these topics. The new Secretary of Education should be directed to propose a strategy for doing just that, on a scale sufficient to the need. Existing programs of research, development, and assistance should be examined as possible sources of funds for these purposes. Professional development is a special case. To build the restructured system will require an enormous amount of professional development and the time in which professionals can take advantage of such a resource. Both cost a lot of money. One of the priorities for the new education secretary should be the development of strategies for dealing with these problems. But here, as elsewhere, there are some existing programs in the Department of Education whose funds can be redirected for this purpose, programs that are not currently informed by the goals that we have spelled out. Much of what we have in mind here can be accomplished through the reauthorization of the Office of Educational Research and Improvement. Legislation for that reauthorization was prepared for the last session of Congress, but did not pass. That legislation was informed by a deep distrust of the Republican administration, rather than the vision put forward by the Clinton campaign. But that can and should be remedied on the next round.

Early Childhood Education
The president-elect has committed himself to a great expansion in the funding of Head Start. We agree. But the design of the program should be changed to reflect several important requirements. The quality of professional preparation for the people who staff these programs is very low and there are no standards that apply to their employment. The same kind of standard setting we have called for in the rest of this plan should inform the approach to this program. Early childhood education should be combined with quality daycare to provide wrap-around programs that enable working parents to drop off their children at the beginning of the workday and pick them up at the end. Full funding for the very poor should be combined with matching funds to extend the tuition paid by middle class parents to make sure that these programs are not officially segregated by income. The growth of the program can be addressed along the way, based on developing examples of best practice. These and other related issues need to be addressed, in our judgement, before the new administration commits itself on the specific form of increased support for Head Start.

Putting the Package Together:
Here we remind you of what we said at the beginning of this letter about timing the legislative agenda. We purpose that you assemble the ideas just described into four high priority packages that will enable you to move quickly on the campaign promises:

1. The first would use your proposal for an apprenticeship system as the keystone of the strategy for putting the whole new postsecondary standards, the Collaborative Design and Development proposal, the technical assistance proposal, and the postsecondary education finance proposal.
2. The second would combine the initiatives on dislocated workers, the rebuilt employment service and the new system of labor market boards as the Clinton administration's employment security program, built on the best practices anywhere in the world. This is the backbone of a system for assuring adult workers in our society that they need never again watch with dismay as their jobs disappear and their chances of ever getting a good job again go with them.
3. The third would concentrate on the overwhelming problems of our inner cities, combining most of the elements of the first and second packages into a special program to greatly raise the work-related skills of the people trapped in the core of our great cities.
4. The fourth would enable you to take advantage of legislation on which Congress has already been working to advance the elementary and secondary reform agenda. It would combine the successor to HR 4323 and S.2 (incorporating the systemic reforms agenda and the board for student performance standards), with the proposal for revamping Chapter 1.

Organizing the Executive Branch for Human Resources Development

The issue here is how to organize the federal government to make sure that the new system is actually built as a seamless web in the field, where it counts, and that program gets a fast start with a first-rate team behind it.

We propose, first, that the President appoint a National

Council on Human Resources Development. It would consist of the relevant key White House officials, cabinet members, and members of Congress. It would also include a small number of governors, educators, business executives, labor leaders, and advocates for minorities and the poor. It would be established in such a way as to assure continuity of membership across administrations, so that the consensus it forges will outlast any one administration. It would be established in such a way as to assure continuity of membership across administrations, so that the consensus it forges will outlast any one administration. It would be charged with recommending broad policy on a national system of human resources development to the President and the Congress, assessing the effectiveness and promise of current programs and proposing new ones. It would be staffed by senior officials on the Domestic Policy Council staff of the President.

Second, we propose that a new agency be created, the National Institute for Learning, Work and Service. Creation of this agency would signal instantly the new administration's commitment to putting the continuing education and training of the "forgotten half" on a par with the preparation of those who have historically been given the resources to go to "college" and to integrate the two systems, not with a view to dragging down the present system and those it serves, but rather to make good on the promise that everyone will have access to the kind of education that only a small minority have had access to up to now. To this agency would be assigned the functions now performed by the assistant secretary for employment and training, the assistant secretary for vocational education and the assistant secretary for higher education. The agency would be staffed by people specifically recruited from all over the country for the purpose. The staff would be small, high powered, and able to move quickly to implement the policy initiatives of the new President in the field of human resources development.

The closest existing model to what we have in mind is the National Science Board and the National Science Foundation, with the council in the place of the board and the institute in the place of the foundation. But our council would be advisory, whereas the board is governing. If you do not like the idea of a permanent council, you might consider the idea of a temporary President's Task Force, constituted much as the council would be.

In this scheme, the Department of Education would be free to focus on putting the new student performance standards in place and managing the programs that will take the leadership in the national restructuring of the schools. Much of the financing and disbursement functions of the higher education program would move to the Treasury Department, leaving the higher education staff in the new institute to focus on matters of substance.

In any case, as you can see, we believe that some extraordinary measure well short of actually merging the departments of labor and education is required to move the new agenda with dispatch.

Getting Consensus on the Vision

Radical changes in attitudes, values, and beliefs are required to move any combination of these agendas. The federal government will have little direct leverage on many of the actors involved. For much of what must be done a new, broad consensus will be required. What role can the new administration play in forging that consensus and how should it go about doing it?

At the narrowest level, the agenda cannot be moved unless there is agreement among the governors, the President, and the Congress. Bill's role at the Charlottesville summit leads naturally to a reconvening of that group, perhaps with the addition of key members of Congress and others.

But we think that having an early summit on the subject of the whole human resources agenda would be risky, for many reasons. Better to build on Bill's enormous success during the campaign with national talk shows, in school gymnasiums, and the bus trips. He could start on the consensus–building progress this way, taking his message directly to the public, while submitting his legislative agenda and working it on the Hill. After six months or so, when the public has warmed to the ideas and the legislative packages are about to get into hearings, then you might consider some form of summit, broadened to include not only the governors, but also key members of Congress and others whose support and influence are important. This way, Bill can be sure that the agenda is his, and he can go into it with a groundswell of support behind him.

That's it. None of us doubt that you have thought long and hard about many of these things and have probably gone way beyond what we have laid out in many areas. But we hope that there is something here that you can use. We would, of course, be very happy to flesh out these ideas at greater length and work with anyone you choose to make them fit the work that you have been doing.

Very best wishes from all of us to you and Bill.

Mark Tucker

End Notes

1. William J. Federer, *Americas God and Country Encyclopedia of Quotations* (Coppell, Texas 1994), p. 282
2. Ibid., p. 281
3. Seth Ames, *Works of Fisher Ames* (Indianapolis, IN: Liberty Classics, 1983), p. xix
4. David Barton, *Education and the Founding Fathers* (Aledo, TX: Wallbuilders, 1993), p. 7
5. Ibid. p. 4
6. Saxe Commins, *Basic Writings of George Washington* (New York: Random House, 1948), p. 356
7. *Journals of Congress (1941)*, Vol. XXIII, p. 572, September 12, 1782.
8. Holy Bible, printed by Robert Aitken and approved by Congress, 1782, preface
9. *Acts Passed at Congress of the United States, March 4, 1789* (Hartford: Hudson and Goodwin, 1791)
10. Benjamin Rush, *Essays, Literary, Moral, and Philosophical* (1806), pp. 93-94
11. Mark Beliles, *Thomas Jeffersons Abridgement of the Words of Jesus of Nazareth,* (Charlottesville, VA: Americans Providential History, 1993), p. 75
12. Ibid.
13. Ibid.
14. Ibid.
15. Ibid.
16. Ibid.

17. Memorandum, University of Virginia, Cabell Hall October 8, 1998
18. Mark Beliles, *Thomas Jeffersons Abridgement of the Words of Jesus of Nazareth*, p. 75
19. David Barton, *Original Intent*, (Aledo, TX: Wallbuilders, 1996), p. 53
20. William Blackstone, *Commentaries on the Laws of England* (1856), Vol. 1 Section II p. 28
21. Ibid., p. 28
22. Ibid., vol. 4, chapter XIV, p. 68
23. Ibid., p. 161
24. Ibid., p. 168.
25. Ibid., pp. 165–166
26. Ibid., p. 166
27. Ibid., p. 166
28. David Barton, *Advice to the Young* (Aledo, TX: Wallbuilders, 1993), p. 11
29. Noah Webster, *Dictionary of the English Language* (Springfield, MA, 1854), p. xxii
30. Ibid., p. xxii
31. David Barton, *Education and the Founding Fathers* (Aledo, TX: Wallbuilders, 1993), pp. 14–15
32. Noah Webster, *History of the United States,* (New Haven, CT, 1836), preface
33. David Barton, *Orginal Intent,* p. 325
34. Ibid., p. 325
35. David Barton, *Keys to Good Government,* (Aledo, TX: Wallbuilders, 1993), pp. 6–7
36. Noah Webster, *History of the United States,* pp. 309–310
37. William Webster, *Speller and Definer* (Philadelphia, PA), inside front cover
38. Kansas Educators and Kansas State Historical Society, *Columbia History of Education in Kansas* (Topeka: Edwin H.

Snow, State Printer, 1893) p 82

39. *Americas Providential History,* (Charlottesville, VA: Providence Foundation, 1994), p 108

40. *Engel v. Vitale,* 370 U.S. 421 (1962)

41. David Barton, *Original Intent,* pp. 45–46

42. *Reynolds v. U.S.,* 98 U.S. 145 (1878)

43. *Congressional Record,* June 7–September 25, 1789, p. 730

44. *Lee v. Weisman,* 112 S. CT. 2649; 120 L. Ed. 2d 467 (1992)

45. *Abington v. Schempp,* 374 U.S. 203 (1963)

46. Ibid., p 209

47. Robert Flood, *The Rebirth of America,* p 127

48. *Stone v. Graham,* 449 U.S. 39 at 42 (1980)

49. *Edwards v. Aquillard,* 482 U.S. 578 (1987)

50. David Barton, *Original Intent,* p. 228

51. David Barton, *America to Pray? or Not to Pray?* (Aledo, TX: Wallbuilders, 1994), p. 58

52. Ibid., p. 76

53. Ibid., p. 78

54. Ibid., p. 78

55. James Dobson, *Family News,* Issue #4, 1998, p. 2

56. David Barton, *America to Pray? or Not to Pray?,* p 26

57. Ibid., p. 29

58. *Washington Post,* June 10, 1997, p. 3

59. David Barton, *America to Pray? or Not to Pray?,* p. 36

60. Ibid., p. 44

61. *New York Times,* May 21, 1997, p. A-1

62. David Barton, *Original Intent,* p. 243

63. David Barton, *America to Pray? or Not to Pray?,* p. 75

64. Ibid., p. 75

65. Ibid., p. 76

66. Ibid., p. 75

67. Ibid., p. 40

68. *USA Today,* March 25, 1998

69. *The New York Times,* May 22, 1998
70. Associated Press, December 16, 1997
71. *Washington Post,* October 22, 1997, p. A3
72. Ibid., April 26, 1998, p. A1
73. Berit Kjos, *Brave New Schools,* (Eugene, OR: Harvest House Publishers, 1995), p. 55
74. Mel and Norma Gabler, *What Are They Teaching Our Children?,* (Longview, TX: Victor Books), p. 91
75. Kurt Billings, *A Generation Deceived* (Solid Rock Books, Inc.), pp. 174–176
76. *Sociological Function of Myths,* SE-179, par. 1, lines 1-2
77. *Psychology for You,* chapter titled "Mythology and Psychology" (Oxford Book Company), SE-189, 1973
78. Ibid., p 191
79. Mel and Normal Gabler, *What Are They Teaching Our Children?,* pp. 39–40
80. Bennett, *Person to Person,* SE-278, col. 1, par. 2, 1981
81. *Special Legistative Report,* Concerned Women for America, Washington D.C., 1997
82. *Americas Providential History,* pp 250–251
83. The Mel Gablers, Report #T-588, 1992
84. *Humanist* magazine, January/February 1983, pp. 25–26
85. *Torcaso v. Watkins,* 367 U.S. 488 (1961)
86. Paul Scott, *The Scott Report,* Washington News–Intelligence Syndicate, January 5, 1972, p. R-10
87. Berit Kjos, *Brave New Schools,* p. 161
88. *Washington Times,* August 21, 1997
89. *The Weekly Standard,* August 19, 1996, p. 21.
90. *Education Newsline* (Costa Mesa, CA: National Association of Christian Educators), Winter 1998, p. 2
91. Ibid., "Presidents Report," July 1997, p. 2
92. *Today, the Bible and You,* January 1988, p. 3
93. Berit Kjos, *Brave New Schools*

94. Marlin Maddoux, *Freedom Club,* February 1997, p 7

95. The eighteen-page letter to Hillary Clinton from the NCEE dated November 11, 1992

96. Kathy Finnegan, *Goals 2000,* (Oklahoma City, OK: Hearthstone Publishing, Ltd., 1996)

97. Ibid., p. 116

98. Ibid., p. 165

99. Berit Kjos, *Brave New Schools,* p. 215

100. *The Oregonian,* June 17, 1994, p. A-1

101. Marlin Maddoux, Point of View interview with Barb Tennison, February 27, 1997

102. Berit Kjos, *Brave New Schools,* p. 220

103. Gary Kah, *Hope for the World,* Spring 1997, p. 1

104. World Constitution and Parliament Association, 8800 West 14th Avenue, Lakewood, CO 80215

105. *A Constitution for the Federation of Earth,* World Constitution and Parliament Association 1991, p. f

106. *World Government,* World Constitution and Parliament Association, October 13, 1992

107. *The World Core Curriculum Manual,* The Robert Muller School, Arlington, TX 76016, 1986

108. Gary Kah, *Hope for the World,* Spring 1997, p. 2

109. Ibid., p 6

110. Ibid., p 6

111. *The World Core Curriculum Manual,* preface